"*Raising a Star* is the best-written, most truthful and informative book on the subject I've ever seen. This isn't just practical tips (though it is all that). This book has soul and, most of all, hope. Nancy Carson has the experience to teach and the heart to help. Read with eyes to see and go change the world."

—Charlie Peacock, producer for Amy Grant and CeCe Winans

"*Raising a Star* is a fantastic and complete guide to helping kids become professional performers. Nancy Carson's wonderful understanding and caring for kids is evident in every page. It is enjoyable to read and full of clear insights and guidance."

—Cynthia Samuelson, owner of Stagedoor Manor Camp and Performing Arts Training Center

"In *Raising a Star* Nancy Carson shares truthful words of practical wisdom. She has years of experience as an agent and really cares about young actors and their families. This is a 'must read' for anyone new to show business."

—Diane Hill Harden, owner of The Young Actor's Space and partner in Hardin/Eckstein Management

"With an absolutely right blend of knowledge, experience, and love for her clients, Nancy Carson has produced a definitive guide for children and teenagers in show business. Parents, easily confused by the maze of information out there, will seize upon this smart, insightful, often amusing trek through the talent-strewn world of entertainment."

—Jules Feiffer, playwright, artist, and author

"Nancy Carson is a rare person in this business, as she'll help your child book performing jobs, but equally important to her is your child's future—that they are happy, healthy, and whole *after* the show has closed. They may work as hard as adults, but she remembers that they are children, first and foremost."

—Kahlua O'Callahan, mother of Julianna Mauriello, star of Nickelodeon's *LazyTown*

RAISING A
Star

ST. MARTIN'S GRIFFIN
NEW YORK

RAISING A

Star

The Parents' Guide to Helping Kids

Break into Theater, Film,

Television, or Music

Nancy Carson

WITH JACQUELINE SHANNON

This book is for informational purposes only. It is not intended to take the place of legal or other professional advice. Readers are advised to consult an attorney or other appropriate professional regarding their own, or their children's, individual situations. Web sites offered as sources of information may have changed or disappeared since this was written, and the listing of a Web site in this book does not mean that the author or publisher endorses any of the information or recommendations contained therein.
In a few instances, when full names have not been used, the individuals described are composites.

www.stmartins.com

Library of Congress Cataloging-in-Publication Data

Carson, Nancy.
Raising a star : the parents' guide to helping kids break into theater, film, television, or music / Nancy Carson with Jacqueline Shannon.—1st ed.
p. cm.
ISBN 0-312-32986-5
EAN 978-0312-32986-0
1. Performing arts—Vocational guidance. 2. Child actors. 3. Child musicians. I. Shannon, Jacqueline. II. Title.

PN1580.C367 2005
791'.023—dc22   2004051248

First Edition: April 2005

10 9 8 7 6 5 4 3 2 1

In memory of

GENE BUSNAR

who convinced me to write a book,

who believed that I could write it, and whose

spirit guided me through the process.

Contents

Acknowledgments

I would first like to thank my literary agent, Linda Konner, and my editor at St. Martin's Press, Becki Heller, for their help and contributions. Thanks also to Jacqueline Shannon for her hard work and hand-holding, especially on the music business chapter.

I am very grateful to all of my friends in the entertainment industry who have given generously of their time to be interviewed. Their insights and expertise have enriched the book greatly.

This book could not exist without all of my Carson-Adler "kids," past and current. It's *their* stories that have brought life to my words. I love them all!

I also want to acknowledge the following for their help and support along the way: my husband, George Davis Harrington; my sons, Stephen and David Deroski; and my granddaughter, Shelly Deroski.

I want to thank my friend Alan Fawcett for conceiving the idea of a book and introducing me to Gene Busnar. This is all his fault.

Finally, a special word of appreciation to Shirley Faison, who works with me at Carson-Adler, and my daughter, Bonnie Deroski, who not only works with me, but also pushed me into the crazy world of show business. Bonnie, this is your book, too!

RAISING A
Star

A Script for Success

In 1994 a family of four sat in my waiting room. Their five-year-old son had been referred to me by another parent. He was a beautiful child who had been featured in a popular Gap print campaign. I invited him into my office to get to know him. He was sweet but a little shy and had a slight French accent, which was not surprising since his father was French and he attended the Lycée Français, a school in New York City. When we finished the **interview** I went out to the waiting room to invite his parents into my office for a chat. That was when I spotted the little boy's older sister. She was just lovely.

Interview:

The first meeting between a performer and any professional involved in the audition process.

"Is she interested in meeting me?" I inquired.

"Well, maybe," her parents told me, "but her teeth are pretty bad, so we didn't think we should pursue show business for her right now."

I encouraged them to let her read a scene from a **script** for me, and they agreed. After she had spent a few minutes working on the lines in my waiting room, I asked her into my office to show what she could do. I couldn't believe her level of naturalness and acting ability. Later, when I spoke with her mother and father, I told them that I didn't think that their son was quite ready for what we do, but that their daughter had the makings of a star. They were somewhat surprised but pleased. That was when they shared with me that their daughter had been pulled out of her classroom by the **casting director** for *Interview with a Vampire*, and although she didn't get the job, the casting director had also told them that she was exceptionally good.

Script:

A production such as a film or play in its written form.

Casting director (casting agent):

A professional employed by a producer or production company to search for the talent needed for a specific project.

I began to send her on **auditions,** and the response was very positive, but that first job is always so hard to get. Finally, she was one of the last two girls in the running for a nice role in the television movie *Reunion* with Marlo Thomas and Peter Strauss. Again, the other, more experienced girl got the job. Then there was an amazing turn of events. It was several days later, over the weekend. My home phone rang, and it was the casting director of *Reunion*, Mary Colquhoun.

Audition:

A tryout during which a performer displays his/her abilities
for an agency, casting director, and/or other professionals.

"Tell me that Leelee Sobieski is wonderful and that she can
handle this job," she begged.

"Of course she is, and of course she can," I responded.
"But why?"

"Because we have an emergency," she told me. "The other little
girl is very sick and can't accept the movie role. I need to hire
someone right away, and I think we'd like to give Leelee a chance."

Reunion was Leelee's first television movie, and it opened the
door into an amazing show business career for her. Leelee went on
to do several more television movies and the feature film *Jungle 2
Jungle* with Tim Allen. She co-starred in the television series *Charlie
Grace* and starred in the Merchant Ivory film *A Soldier's Daughter
Never Cries* as well as in several other feature films while still a
young teenager. From there Leelee reached heights not even I
could have imagined. Her Emmy-nominated role as Joan of Arc
in the television miniseries of the same name was finished before
she had even graduated from high school. However, there was
never any question in my mind that the raw talent and other ingredients were there from the start for her. There always has to be
a beginning for every major star.

In order to help a young person and her family reach anything
like this level of success, it takes a tremendous amount of time,
effort, and individual guidance on my part. Unfortunately, there
aren't enough hours in the day to give this kind of personal attention to every child and parent who needs it. I've often wished that

I could hand people a book and say, "Read this from cover to cover before you take a step or spend one penny." How much confusion and anxiety they could avoid; how much easier my job would be. Since I've never been able to find that book, I decided to write it myself.

As an **agent,** I'm right at the heart of this business every day, dealing with parents, young performers, and the professionals who hire them. I've seen so many talented young people out there who could be fulfilling themselves and earning money—if only their parents knew the right steps to take. This book is intended to help you decide whether your child is right for one or more of the performing fields, and to show you how to best prepare him or her for local work, major auditions, and eventual success.

Agent:

A professional who represents, advises, solicits work for, and negotiates on behalf of a performer for a commission.

Thousands of boys and girls from all over the country carve out lucrative careers for themselves without having any previous track record, tremendous financial resources, or special connections in the business. Like Leelee, most of these successful young performers have supportive families and experienced professionals on their side. But even the greatest parents and most powerful agent can't do much if a young performer doesn't start out with the right basic ingredients.

Here are ten qualities that many top child performers have. While it's not absolutely necessary for your son or daughter to possess every attribute in equal measure, the prospects are far better when most of these signs are there:

Ten Qualities Successful Young
Performers Possess

1. Motivation
2. A winning look
3. Talent
4. Reading ability and a good memory
5. Verbal skills
6. Natural expressive abilities
7. Imagination
8. Independence
9. Well-rounded interests
10. Ability to handle pressure and rejection

Motivation

Who wants a show business career more, you or your child? Whatever else a youngster has going for him, nothing is more important than his own burning desire to perform professionally. A motivated child will let you know how he feels. He will look at a television commercial and tell you, "I think I can do that; I want to do that." He'll ask you if he can be in the school play; he may even write his own play and produce it in the back yard.

The child I'm looking for is the one who drags her parent into the office, not the reverse. When a parent says to his daughter, "Go on this audition and I'll get you a new bicycle," I know we're in trouble. Girls and boys who really want a performing career don't have to be bribed. As the saying goes, "It's in their blood."

There are countless stories about pushy stage mothers and fathers who are determined to make their children stars at all costs. In my daily work I've witnessed more tragic and funny scenarios than you could imagine. But I know from personal experience that a parent's desire to override a child's own wishes is no laughing matter.

When my son Stephen was in his early teens, he began working in commercials. Stephen had been featured in commercials for Colgate, Tang, and Milton Bradley. He was also in several plays, including the Broadway production of *The Shadow Box*. Stephen's career seemed to be going very well and his services were in great demand. There was just one problem—he hated auditioning. Once he got the job, he liked the work. But it became an unbearable chore for Stephen to go on auditions. One day he walked up to me and said, "Mom, I just don't want to do this anymore. I want to stop."

I must admit that I didn't take this news very well. Frankly, I liked the idea that my son was attractive and special enough to be working in high-paying commercials. At first I just couldn't accept his decision to throw this opportunity away. But after talking it over with Stephen, I realized that the choice wasn't mine to make.

I'm proud to report that Stephen has since graduated from Rutgers University and is working as a science teacher in California. But shortly after he gave up show business, I was pretty upset. Instead of pocketing substantial sums filming TV commercials, Stephen was earning extra money in such unglamorous, low-paying jobs as a deli cashier and record store clerk. Stephen has no regrets at all about bowing out of show business. And all things considered, neither do I.

Now let's look at the other side of the coin—at the kind of young person who wants nothing more than to be a performer.

One day I received a phone call from an eleven-year-old boy named Ramzi Khalaf.

"I read a magazine article about you," Ramzi said, "and I want to make an appointment to come and see you about becoming an actor."

"Do your parents know you're calling me?" I asked.

"Not yet," he answered. "I was planning on telling them."

I said, "You're going to have to have your parents call to set up the appointment."

The next day, Ramzi's mother called and said, "Our son keeps bothering us to make an appointment to come see you. Ramzi has this crazy idea that he wants to be an actor, and we can't seem to talk him out of it."

I was so intrigued by the young man's initiative and desire that I agreed to meet with Ramzi and his parents. Both parents were professors at Princeton University. They knew absolutely nothing about show business, and clearly they were hoping I'd talk their son out of it. But it soon became obvious that I didn't need to talk Ramzi out of becoming a performer; I needed to talk his parents *into* it. The young man clearly had the talent, and wanted to be a performer more than anything in the world. When I told Ramzi's parents that I wanted to represent him, they were visibly disappointed.

"Please, Mom, Dad, this is what I need to do!" Ramzi said. "You must let me try." The parents finally relented, but they were not pleased.

I immediately started sending Ramzi out on auditions. Within three weeks, he landed a role in the Broadway production of *Falsettos*. He went on to do *A Christmas Carol*, and created the role of Young Scrooge. Ramzi continued to work regularly. But suddenly there was a major change in the family's situation.

The city of Beirut was beginning to be rebuilt, and the American University invited Ramzi's father to teach there. The Khalafs felt an obligation to return to their country of origin, and insisted that their son go with them. In Beirut, Ramzi felt miserable and lonely, unable to work at what he felt he was born to do. Eventually the young man convinced his parents to let him come back to New York, live with close friends, and finish high school there. I immediately began to send him out on auditions, and he quickly started landing commercials and theatrical roles.

At this writing, Ramzi is completing his studies at New York University. There's no question in my mind that Ramzi will be able to sustain a show business career as an adult, in large part because of his extraordinary motivation.

A Winning Look

Mothers and fathers often ask if their son or daughter has to be beautiful in order to succeed in show business. As a matter of fact, some of my most successful kids are not at all good-looking in a conventional sense. But all of them have a winning look, something unique that makes them stand out from the crowd.

Some kids have a winning look because they're able to draw attention to themselves without being conventionally good-looking. One of my young clients, Nicolas King, was the star of a long-running commercial for Lunchables. He was also in several Broadway shows, including *A Thousand Clowns* and *Hollywood Arms*. Nick is actually kind of offbeat-looking by conventional standards, but he's so adorable you can't take your eyes off him.

Though there are few hard-and-fast rules, certain looks are easier for agents to sell than others. All things being equal, a small child has a better chance than one who is big for her age. A ten-year-old who looks fourteen may have a hard time competing against more seasoned performers, while a ten-year-old who looks eight has a decided advantage when she goes up against younger kids.

A good example is Haley Joel Osment. While he played approximately eight years old in *The Sixth Sense*, with Bruce Willis, he was actually pushing eleven. More recently, he starred in *Secondhand Lions* with Michael Caine and Robert Duvall, again playing a prepubescent boy, though he was actually fourteen or fifteen at the time of filming. Typically, young actors tend to drop out of sight for a few years when they reach the awkward puberty stage (think Fred Savage of TV's *The Wonder Years*). After this limbo, they may or may not return to acting. If they do, they face a new age competition. Young adults who can pass as teenagers are highly valued because of their mental maturity and their availability. They are not subject to child labor restrictions or required to go to school. Examples include Amber Tamblyn, who was twenty but passing as sixteen when she started her TV series *Joan of Arcadia,* and Gabrielle Carteris, who played Andrea on *Beverly Hills 90210.* When that series about affluent teens first went on the air, Gabrielle was an astonishing twenty-nine years old.

The looks of show business children reflect popular tastes and styles. That's why buck teeth, jug-handle ears, and big noses are not usually sought-after qualities. Even so, certain children have an appealing and saleable look in spite of—and in some cases because of—their imperfections. I have several kids with such features who work regularly because casting directors think they look real. Sometimes youngsters with special features are needed to emphasize a particular message. In such cases, **directors** want these characteristics to be exaggerated, not subtle. A chubby child, for example, may not have as much potential for working as one who is downright obese. That's because if a director wants fat, he usually wants really fat, not just chunky.

Director:

The person who is generally responsible for the artistic quality of a production, including the actors' performances, the interpretation of the script, and the general overseeing of the technical aspects of the production.

Situations involving race and ethnic origin can sometimes stretch the question of physical **type** into delicate and complex areas. Although we still have a long way to go, I'm happy to say that things are so much more open than they were even five or ten years ago. The demand for children of color has been growing by leaps and bounds. Producers and directors now seem more willing to overlook traditional stereotypes for the sake of talent. This trend toward nontraditional casting is a very positive development.

Type:

The personality and look of a performer.

Talent

Every community has its share of talented kids, but just how much ability does a child need to make it professionally? Talent in any field is a relative commodity. For example, a great high school athlete often isn't good enough to make his college team—just as many college all-Americans don't measure up as professionals. As you move up through the ranks in any field, the competition invariably becomes tougher. So if your child hasn't been able to land a part at the local dinner theater, ask yourself how he's likely to fare at a Broadway audition. On the other hand, it doesn't necessarily follow that a young person who is the best singer or actress in her school district has what it takes to make it as a professional.

It's sometimes difficult for mothers and fathers to be objective about their child's talent, especially when that boy or girl is dressed in an adorable costume, standing in the spotlight in the school play. But when knowledgeable people make a point of telling you—without your asking—that your child has exceptional ability, that is usually a far more reliable indication.

The self-proclaimed "record producer" who says your child is the next Mariah Carey and then asks you to contribute to the cost of making a pricey demo in a state-of-the-art recording facility is someone you should ignore. The same goes for the modeling agent who wants you to spend thousands of dollars on expensive photos. The best judges of talent are seasoned professionals who don't stand to benefit from making false promises.

Possible Signs That a Young Performer Has Talent

- A cousin who has ignored you for years asks your son to perform at her wedding.
- Community theaters seek out your daughter for their productions, even though you've never offered them financial support.
- Your daughter's dance teacher calls to say that she has what it takes to work professionally, without also suggesting that she needs additional lessons and costumes.
- Your son's teacher calls you in the evening—and this time it's to tell you that he was fantastic in the school play.
- Your son is asked to sing a solo in every performance of the church choir, even though you and the choir director can't stand each other.

As an agent, I have everything to lose when I miscalculate a performer's ability. I only make money if a performer lands a job. Therefore, if I tell a parent that her child has talent, I'm effectively promising to devote my time and other resources to developing and marketing that natural ability. Other show business pros, like directors and casting agents, are also credible judges of talent. But even the best and most experienced professionals can sometimes make a wrong call.

Ben Affleck became my client when he was fifteen. One of the first auditions I sent him out on was for a major comedy film. Afterward, the director called to say, "This kid has talent, but he just can't handle comedy. He read his lines just fine, but there's absolutely nothing funny about this guy."

Over the years, Ben has received rave notices for his starring work in such comedy hits as *Shakespeare in Love, Dogma,* and *Chasing Amy.* Incidents like this bring home how wrong a particular talent evaluator can be on any given day. That's why you always want to solicit more than one professional opinion and base your conclusion on a consensus of the feedback.

Reading Ability and a Good Memory

At acting auditions, young actors are typically handed a script and asked to read it on the spot. If someone interests me at an initial interview, I test him in much the same way a casting director would. First I hand the child some **sides** and ask him to look them over for a few minutes; then I have him read for me. The following is an example of the kind of commercial script I often use with boys and girls between the ages of seven and twelve.

My mom's the best cook in the world. And I know 'cause I just spent a week with Aunt Bernice, and when she makes chicken it comes out "yuk." But Mom makes chicken with Shake 'n' Chicken, so it comes out all crispy on top and juicy in the middle. See, my mom knows it's the only way I like it. That's why my mom's the best cook in the world. I'm glad Aunt Bernice isn't my mom.

Sides:

An incomplete script that shows only the lines and cues of a single performer.

What I'm looking for here is the child who can read convincingly. I want to feel that he really hates his Aunt Bernice's chicken and loves his mom's. The way a child reads a piece of **commercial copy** also gives me an idea of how he'll handle longer scripts. Children who can read quickly for meaning and render their lines with personality and expression have a decided edge.

Commercial copy:

The script for a radio or television commercial.

If a child makes it to the final audition for television or film, he may be asked to memorize the script and put it on videotape. In addition, performers must be able to remember a complex sequence of orders given by a director. If it comes down to a choice between two children who are equal in other respects, the faster memorizer and the better reader will usually land the part.

One question I'm often asked concerns the prospects for children with dyslexia and other reading deficits. I have worked successfully with talented young performers who have had reading problems, and I'm open to doing so in the future—if that performer possesses most of the other attributes I'm looking for. As much as possible, I try to get a copy of the sides in advance, so that the young person can memorize the lines prior to the audition. Several Hollywood superstars are reputed to be dyslexic, which is an open secret in the industry. In any event, the good news is that if a performer can really act, there are things he and his agent can do to overcome most reading difficulties.

Verbal Skills

Children who perform well are usually good talkers. If I ask a verbal child who walks into my office for the first time, "How was your trip?" she won't just say, "Fine." Instead, the child will often say something like, "We came by car, and there was lots of traffic in the tunnel. That always seems to happen whenever we come into the city on a Friday."

Verbal children like to tell stories that tend to be well-organized and highly animated. Many of these verbal, outgoing children are also surprisingly good listeners. Instead of monopolizing the conversation, they try to hear what you're saying and respond appropriately. This is an important asset, since all performers must learn to take direction.

Young people who speak clearly and without any foreign accent, regional dialect, or speech impediment are easiest to sell. A child's accent or use of regional slang might occasionally turn in his favor if someone is looking for that particular type. But there is more work available for young performers who are versatile. If you can only sound like a kid who comes from New England, for example, you can only play roles that call for that kind of regionalism. Few young performers can find enough work when their speech so narrowly pigeonholes them.

Because I'm based in the New York City area, I meet a lot of people with heavy Bronx or Brooklyn accents. One of my clients, Frankie Galasso, is a kid from the Bronx who has done a bunch of TV and was part of the vocal group Dream Street. Frankie has learned to speak in a nonregional dialect, but his mother still talks with a heavy Bronx accent. It took me a while to convince her that it was in everyone's best interest for her to say as little as possible when she accompanies Frankie on auditions. That advice extends to all parents whose speech has a regional or foreign flavor.

Kids who lisp and stutter often have a harder time than those with regional accents. However, many of these speech-related dif-ficulties can be cleared up fairly easily. If a child has a speech problem but everything else seems right, it might be worthwhile to try to correct it. A slight lisp on a five-year-old isn't going to hurt (in some situations it might even be considered kind of cute). However, a ten-year-old with a lisp is going to have a hard time.

Natural Expressive Abilities

One of the things I hear over and over again from parents whose kids are unable or unwilling to perform in my office is, "She isn't that way at home," or, "He isn't that way once he gets to know you." Sorry, but the professionals who audition young performers simply don't have time to get to know each child who auditions for them.

Children who are cut out for this business have the ability to be open and natural on demand, even if they're not noticeably extroverted. There's a big difference between vying for attention at school or at home and having the ability to perform in a profes-sional context. Many of my successful clients are reserved in their everyday interactions, but all of them are immediately relaxed and natural in performing situations.

Natural communicators reveal themselves in many ways. They make expressive gestures with their hands or their eyes to communicate. When they read a script, these youngsters are loose enough to perform it for you with their entire bodies.

If a child comes into my office and gives a stiff reading, I'll often say something like, "Reading well in school means reciting the words correctly, but good actors take reading a step further by using their whole bodies to tell the story. We talk with all the parts of our bodies, not just our mouths. Can you show me you're happy or sad without using any words?"

Some children are able to respond immediately, while others seem to have no idea what I'm talking about. The children who do respond are the natural communicators. Parents sometimes ask if lessons are helpful in this area. Frankly, I'm not aware of any kind of training that can take the place of a child's inherent, natural ability to communicate feelings and emotions nonverbally.

Imagination

Performers need a vivid sense of fantasy to imagine themselves as different people in a variety of situations. That's why children who pretend easily often do well in this business.

When my daughter Bonnie was young, she read about Helen Keller. For several days, Bonnie walked around with her eyes shut, holding her ears, pretending that she was blind and deaf. No matter how hard people tried to get through, Bonnie wouldn't acknowledge that she saw or heard anything. Her behavior was terribly frustrating for me as a parent, but I came to understand that it was a sign that she has the ability to become other people.

An early indication of acting talent can be when a very young child makes up imaginary characters who sit at the dinner table and carry on conversations. As with my daughter, Bonnie, such seemingly silly and immature behavior can mean that your child has the vivid imagination and role-playing skills that many successful performers possess.

Independence

One of the things I look for when I first meet a child is an ease and confidence in separating from his or her parent. To do well in this business, a child must be comfortable when relating to strangers. I know I'll have problems if any of these things happen at a first meeting:

- A child won't come into my office without a parent
- A parent won't let the child answer for himself
- A parent refuses to leave her child alone with me
- A child is unable to pretend that someone else is the parent in a role-playing situation

No matter how talented and beautiful a boy or girl is, the interview is over if we can't overcome these hurdles. It's not unusual for a youngster to be nervous and want to hold onto his parent when he first meets a stranger—particularly someone who's going to audition him. When this happens in my office, I'll usually say something like, "If you're on television, Mommy is going to have to wait in the other room, too, so you'll have to get used to it." If the child still doesn't respond, we're through at that point.

Parents have to accept that young performers are, for the most part, treated as adults. Directors simply are not going to stand for a clinging mother or an overly dependent child. Part of my job is to spot these problems before I actually send someone out on an audition.

Well-Rounded Interests

After you've been around them for a while, you realize that successful child performers are in most respects no different from others in their age group. That's why it should come as no surprise that these kids are usually happiest when they can participate in the same activities that their nonperforming friends enjoy.

Most of my clients are very bright and extremely well-rounded. For example, Anthony Blair Hall (*Ragtime, A Christmas Carol*) is a champion wrestler on his high school team. Genia Micheala (the Broadway production of *The Crucible* and television's *Max Bickford*) is an Olympic-level women's ice hockey player. Frankie Galasso is so involved in sports that I have had to schedule auditions around his games.

Though there are occasional scheduling clashes between professional and nonperforming activities, I strongly encourage mothers and fathers to support their children in pursuing a wide variety of interests outside of show business. This is particularly important after a young performer achieves a degree of success and recognition.

There's another, less obvious reason to help young performers lead normal, well-rounded lives. Most of the kids I work with have a fresh, natural quality that attracts me when we first meet. When children get too caught up in show-biz glitz, they often lose much of that freshness. This can hurt them as people, and it can also cause them to lose some of the winning qualities that helped make them successful in the first place.

Ability to Handle Pressure and Rejection

If your child has all the attributes we've been discussing to this point, chances of securing work are excellent. But if he can't handle the pressures of a fast-paced, high-stakes, adult business, his career will be short-lived.

Because show business is a business, children may be required to deal with situations that would try the emotions of even the most emotionally stable grownup. If your child has ever come home crying after being dumped from her school play or benched by his soccer coach, ask yourself how he or she might deal with the kind of rejection my clients come up against on a regular basis. I have many stories to share in this regard, but the best and most poignant concerns two young clients who are now college graduates.

In a Broadway production of *Oliver!* nine of the children were clients of mine, including a talented eleven-year-old actor named Cameron Johann. Originally, the show's associate director had selected Cameron for the lead role. A few weeks before the show was to open, the **producer** and director arrived from England and walked into a **rehearsal**, never actually having seen their Oliver. Several hours later I received a phone call:

Producer:

The person who generally coordinates and supervises all facets of a particular production.

—In theater: the person who arranges for the staging of a dramatic work, including the financing and management.

—In film and video: the person who prepares a program for broadcast and is therefore responsible for its economic success.

Rehearsal:

A practice session to prepare a production for public performance.

"Cameron doesn't look enough like an 'Oliver,'" I was told. "He must be replaced."

Cameron had signed a six-month contract, so neither he nor I stood to lose any money because he'd be paid whether he was in the production or not. What concerned me, though, was how the child and his family would handle this terrible disappointment. I tried to soften the blow by insisting that the producers keep him on as an **understudy** and a member of "Fagin's Gang." I also worked out an agreement under which Cameron would actually appear in the show as "Oliver" at a predetermined date. Still, I felt a great big lump in my stomach every time I thought about telling Cameron and his parents that he was not going to play the lead role.

Understudy:

In a theatrical production, an actor, dancer, and/or singer who may be called upon to substitute for the principal performer when needed.

The day all this happened, Cameron's picture had appeared in the New York *Daily News* with star billing. This was not going to be one of my happier days as an agent. First I talked to the parents. They reacted badly, saying that they would sooner take their son home and forget the whole incident. They weren't at all interested in the understudy and **ensemble** parts after Cameron had been slated for the lead. I thoroughly disagreed with their reasoning.

Ensemble:

A group of persons (as a chorus) acting together to produce a particular effect or end.

"You can't do that," I told the Johanns. "That's like running away with your tail between your legs. It's very important for Cameron to get back on that horse and ride again after being thrown." I finally convinced them that it would be best for Cameron to stay with the show, but the hardest part was still ahead: We had to break the news to the child.

The Johanns and I went over to the theater and pulled Cameron out of rehearsal. When he heard the news, he cried and cried. He kept saying, "No, no, I want to go home." Then I talked to him alone.

"Are you going to let them beat you, or are you going to stay here and fight and show these people what you can do? Suppose I had originally told you that they wanted you for 'Fagin's Gang' and to understudy 'Oliver'?" I asked him. "How would you have felt?" Cameron admitted that he would have been really happy. I pointed out that he was still a very important part of the show. "Can't you still feel happy?" I pleaded.

After a while Cameron got his fight back and agreed to stay on. We cleaned him up, washed his face, and he walked back into rehearsal. There wasn't a dry eye in that rehearsal hall. I'm really proud of him because I know that many adult performers wouldn't have had the strength to make such a mature decision. But I know that Cameron did the right thing. Next time something traumatic happens, he'll have the strength and confidence to deal with it.

Another delicate aspect of this story is that Braden Danner, the boy ultimately picked to play "Oliver," is also a client of mine. The night after he and Cameron changed places in the ensemble,

Braden called me and said, "Nancy, I want to feel happy, but I feel sad." When I asked why, he replied, "Because Cameron is my friend. He was my first friend in the show. I feel sad for him, and I don't know if I should feel happy for me." I said, "You didn't make the decision—somebody else did." In his own way Braden showed as much strength and maturity in the situation as did Cameron. Instead of gloating over his own good luck, he was able to empathize with another's misfortune. In fact, all the children in the cast became extremely protective of Cameron because they were so proud of how he had behaved in the face of adversity.

Though Cameron certainly showed tremendous grace under pressure for one so young, he never could have done it without the support of those around him. The people surrounding a young performer can make a tremendous difference not only in how he responds to pressure, but also in how he turns out as an adult. In this case, everyone did their respective jobs well. The proof, as the saying goes, is in the pudding.

Cameron Johann and Braden Danner both went on to have very successful performing careers into their late teens. Cameron is a graduate of NYU Film School and Braden is a graduate of the USC Film School. It's interesting that both young men want to be filmmakers. But what makes me proudest is that they've both grown up to become wonderful, well-rounded adults. There's no question in my mind that their experiences as young performers—including the rejection and heartaches—have contributed to making them the quality people they are today.

In chapter 2, I explore the parent's role in helping to make show business a positive and fulfilling experience for a child. But first I'd like you to take a few moments to review the major points we've discussed by answering the following questionnaire. A child's ultimate success will depend on how all his qualities merge into a complete personality. In general, the more *yes* answers you can honestly give, the greater your son or daughter's chances.

Assessing a Young Performer's Chances

1. Has your child ever told you that he or she wants to be in show business?
2. Does your child drag you to see new movies or plays?
3. Do people tend to notice your child when you're out in public?
4. Is your child small for his or her age?
5. Does your child sing or dance extremely well?
6. Do knowledgeable people frequently tell you that your child has outstanding ability?
7. Does your child enjoy reading?
8. Does your child read expressively?
9. Does your child have a good memory?
10. Does your child follow directions well?
11. Does your child express herself well verbally?
12. Does your child have clear, nonregional speech?
13. Is your child outgoing?
14. Is your child imaginative and creative in his or her play?
15. Is your child self-sufficient?
16. Is your child comfortable around strangers?
17. Does your child handle rejection well?
18. Does your child do well in competitive situations?
19. Do you consider your child to be well-rounded?
20. Do you think that a show business career would have a positive impact on your child's future?

2

How You Can Help Your Child Succeed

Once I interview a child and decide that he or she has the qualities I'm looking for, my next interview is with the parents. I've found that even the most talented child cannot succeed in this business without an understanding, cooperative family. If parents' expectations are too unrealistic; if I sense that their motivation is based more on their own needs than on the child's; or if for any other reason I think a family will be especially difficult to work with, I'll turn down even the most talented child. Thousands of boys and girls have the potential to work professionally. Whether they will or not depends, in large part, on you.

Eight Ways You Can Help Your Child Succeed

1. Take the lead from your child
2. Always be supportive
3. Handle your money carefully
4. Make yourself available
5. Stay flexible
6. Learn to roll with the punches
7. Get the whole family into the act
8. Keep a healthy perspective on your child's success

Take the Lead from Your Child

The kind of parent I'm looking for is the one who follows her child's lead. She's become involved in show business for the child, not herself. I know I'll have problems when I meet a mother or father who makes show business the most important thing in the world. Most of the good show business parents I've met support their kids in all kinds of activities—be it Little League, Girl Scouts, or dance lessons. Their child's show business career may be important, but it's only one part of a full life.

Because of the high visibility and big bucks associated with show business, parents sometimes have a hard time keeping their perspective. But to me the situation is not all that different when parents want to get their academically talented child into a good school.

If you live in a large city, for example, and you don't have enough money for a private school, you might make it your goal to try to get your child into a public school for academically gifted students. Since you know that the competition is fierce, you start preparing when he's in the fourth or fifth grade. You might go out and buy books years ahead of time so that he can pass the difficult admissions test. Some people might consider this excessive, but you know that down the road your planning could mean a scholarship to a top college.

That's the same kind of focus and commitment that you might want to put into motion if your child happens to be a gifted performer. Whatever the field, though, the important thing to keep in mind is that your actions should be based on your child's talents and desires, not on your expectations.

Any child with a gift or a talent—whether it be in academics, athletics, or one of the performing arts—is going to need special attention. If your child is a gifted scholar, he's going to require special schools and classes. If he shows tremendous promise athletically, you're going to try to find situations that bring out those talents. The point is this: *If you really want to help your child, let him set the pace.* You need to monitor his physical and emotional states, certainly. But even if he seems at times to be overwhelmed or exhausted by his various activities, *he* needs to make the decision about what to give up.

Always Be Supportive

One of the first evaluations I make of prospective parents is: Are they doing this for themselves or for their child? All children need to feel that you love them not just because they're cute and wonderful and an agent wants to see them. They want you to love them for who they are. If you base your love on what your child does or doesn't accomplish in show business, he's going to have a very difficult time emotionally.

My agency looks for children with supportive families, and I'm happy to say that the vast majority of our clients are emotionally healthy and well-rounded. Still, sometimes I have to remind parents that their child is wonderful for himself, not because he's a wonderful performer who makes the parent look great.

Of course, you can hardly help feeling proud when your child accomplishes something, and there's nothing wrong with that. If you're a father whose son just got straight As on his report card, you'd probably tell everyone in the office. Why should it be any different if your son lands a commercial that two hundred other children were competing for?

Disappointment is often a more delicate matter than success— particularly in competitive fields involving high stakes. We've all seen stage mothers and Little League fathers who look at their kids as if they were some kind of lottery ticket or brass ring. Such misguided parents try to live out their fantasies of wealth and glory through their children. I find such situations tragic. Yet in a way, they are just exaggerations of tendencies that many of us have.

It's only natural to be partial to things that belong to us. Somewhere inside, people tend to feel, "My child is special, so I must be special." It's also easy to feel this way about your pet and even your car: "I have the most beautiful dog or the greatest car. Since my possessions are great," the reasoning goes, "that makes me great."

We've all had feelings like this at one time or another. But thinking about your child in this way is a far more serious matter. Children know whether they're making you feel happy or disappointed. It's okay to feel disappointed *for* the child if she doesn't get the role, but if you're disappointed *in* the child, she's going to know that and feel very hurt. That's why it's so important that you understand your role as that of a helper—someone who is there to support your child in achieving her dreams.

Handle Your Money Carefully

One of the things parents most often ask is, "Do I have to be fabulously wealthy to launch my child's show business career?" The answer is an emphatic *no*. If you know what you're doing, it doesn't have to cost a lot of money.

It's a mistake to think that you have to be rich for your child to have a career in show business. Most successful young performers are from middle-class homes. Some of my clients do come from professional families, but many others are from blue-collar backgrounds. Each family has to decide how much money they have available to launch their child's performing career. But if you believe in your child, trust your agent, and manage your money carefully, you can usually find a way.

In terms of initial expenses, there's really not much more you have to think about beyond a very modest investment in photos and clothing. (In chapter 4 we will fully discuss the most intelligent and cost-effective ways to handle these expenses.) When you start out on the local level, your major expense is transportation. But even this can be kept to a minimum if you have the time to take your child to and from auditions and performances yourself.

Once your child starts earning money locally, it's important that you use that money to finance the expansion of his or her career. If you're not rich, you might be tempted to use the money to pay general household bills. I think that approach is shortsighted.

One of the most talented children I've ever met comes from a poor New Hampshire family. This little girl, whom we'll call Alice, is so exceptional that I've sometimes paid part of her carfare and let her sleep in my extra bedroom. Her parents have a lot of financial difficulties. They have four children, one of whom is learning-disabled and needs special schooling. Because money is so tight, Alice's parents use all the money she earns to pay their mortgage and medical expenses.

These parents have a heavy burden, and I empathize with them. Still, I think they're making a terrible mistake by not using most of the money Alice earns to help support her career. If her parents would only see things in this light, Alice would be doing extremely well. As it is, she can't pursue her promising career beyond the local level. It really breaks my heart to see such a gifted and motivated child held back in this way.

If your child has talent and wants to be a performer, it's going to take a commitment on your part to make it happen. The same kind of commitment is equally important in other fields that require special talents. You don't become a neurosurgeon or a professional athlete overnight. I think that people sometimes forget that a show business career takes that same kind of planning and dedication. When you help your child in this way, you are making an investment in his future. He's getting a head start on his career and an opportunity to do something he really wants to do.

If you want to help your child get started but don't have a lot of money, there are some alternatives you might want to look into. Grandparents are often willing to lend a helping hand. Instead of giving Suzie an expensive Christmas present, they can use that money to finance lessons or trips to auditions. Don't expect others to help, however, if you're not doing all you can do.

Families with modest means may have a difficult decision to make when the time comes to go to a **major market**, where the opportunities are so much greater. It's not cheap to travel from, say, Omaha, Nebraska, to New York for an audition. Spending that money is a gamble, but you can also look at it as a measure of your commitment to your child's future.

Major market:
A large city that supports a variety of professional productions. In general usage, referring to New York, Los Angeles, or Chicago.

Every family has to weigh the financial commitment to the child's performing career against a number of other factors. Two important things to consider are how far you live from the city and your mode of transportation. If you're going to have to ride all night on a bus to take your child to an audition in the morning, forget it. The child is going to be exhausted, you're going to be exhausted, and the audition is not going to go well. If you and your child are going to be under tremendous pressure because this is the only trip you can afford, I suggest that you stay home. Your child's chances are too slim, and there's far too much pressure on everyone concerned.

But let's paint a slightly different picture: Say your money is tight but you want to give it a shot. Then you try to find a bargain flight and keep your other expenses down. There are bed-and-breakfast services that offer inexpensive lodging. Perhaps you have a friend or relative who will put you up for a night or two. One of the better New York hotels offers considerable discounts to actors. You can also save money by eating at inexpensive places. Most kids like to eat at McDonald's at home, so why not eat at McDonald's while you're in the city? If you're careful, you can keep the costs down considerably. Still, traveling to other cities—especially by plane—is not going to be cheap.

As I said earlier, the majority of children who make it in this business don't come from rich families. Many parents have to struggle and make sacrifices. But if you're committed, you can find a way to make it work. Think of how expensive it can be to send a child to summer camp. If you have a son or daughter who wants to work in show business, why not invest that summer camp money in his or her career? You might even consider renting an apartment in New York or Los Angeles for the summer. This would allow your child to attend many more auditions, and it probably would cost less than a good summer camp.

I remember a little eight-year-old girl from Louisiana. She had auditioned for the updated version of *The Mickey Mouse Club* in 1990 and the casting director, Matt Casella, thought she was talented but not ready and not old enough. The parents were anxious to help her but were not sure what to do next. Their finances were tight. They had an older son and a baby on the way. But they still knew they had to help their daughter take the next step. Matt gave them my information and let me know to expect to hear from them. They sent me a letter with some snapshots and a home video done at her dance school. Well, there was no question that this little girl had enormous talent and potential. She just needed some professionals to help her put it all together.

I called the parents and suggested that they think about a trip to New York so that I could meet her in person. To save money, they drove from Louisiana, a long trip for such a little girl. She sang for me in the office and danced in the hall. I gave her a script to read. Though she had no experience at all, it was still clear that this was a star in the making. I introduced the family to the Broadway Dance Center right around the corner from me and a voice teacher familiar with young voices. I told them about vocal coach Robert Marks. Then I asked the big question: Would they think about spending some time in the city so that she could work on her skills and begin to audition?

The family went back to Louisiana. Mom had a baby girl. Then I had a phone call from them. They had decided to try it. I was overjoyed. The little girl could do it, given the chance. They settled in New York and she began to study. We talked about her Southern dialect and I teased her about how "Yes, ma'am" was a dead giveaway.

She auditioned, but nothing happened right away. They began to get discouraged, but I urged them not to give up. Soon she landed a little commercial or two. Then she booked an acting part on *Candid Camera*, and the ice seemed to be broken. With the material she had developed working with the professionals, she was accepted for *Junior Star Search* and just missed the top prize. She was on her way.

Money was still very tight, and it was hard for the family to be separated. I wouldn't have blamed them if they had given up. But they stuck with it because the child wanted it so much. Soon her next break happened. She landed a small part and the understudy for the starring role in an off-Broadway show, *Ruthless*. It wasn't long before she took over the lead role and was singing and dancing on stage in New York City. I'll never forget the excitement that night.

But soon the excitement waned. Christmas was near and she and her mom and baby sister were ready to be back in Louisiana with the family. "We're going home," they said. "You have to help us leave the show." I pulled some strings and hugged them good-bye. It was hard, but I knew it was right for their family. She had sharpened her skills and become a professional. Now we had to wait for the right project to come along and the family needed to be together.

The phone in my office rang one day and it was Matt Casella. "I'm adding some Mouseketeers to the Mouse Club," he said. "Who do you have?" I gave him some suggestions and then, saving the best for last, I asked, "Do you remember the little girl from Louisiana who you sent to me a few years ago? She's the right age and she's ready now." She got her mouse ears that day and the rest of the story is history. That little girl was Britney Spears, and she finally had her big break.

When I first met Britney, she really wasn't quite ready to land major roles. Still, I recognized her potential and encouraged her family to take the plunge. Part of an agent's job is to help you make those difficult financial decisions. Sometimes I'll call a parent and say, "Well, your odds are pretty good on this one. They're looking for Jessica's personality and physical type. The producer really seems to like her. The chances are good." They'll often reply, "I have to look at my budget to see if I can do it. I'll call you back." Most of the time they'll call back and say, "Okay, let's go for it."

Since it can take six months or more for even the most talented child to land a paying job, you have to put aside enough money to sustain the expense of those auditions for that period of time. If the child goes for a while without landing any jobs, you must trust your agent to give you the right advice. She might tell you that the prospects aren't as good as she originally thought. On the other hand, she might say, "Don't give up. I expected it to take some time. Daniel didn't get the part, but I got excellent feedback from the casting director. Let's keep going."

Many families take the plunge, then are tempted to quit. Finally, *boom*, they make it. One of my clients, Ramya Pratt, was just about ready to throw in the towel. I remember how discouraged her parents were. "Maybe we should give up," they said. "Maybe she'll never make it." But I urged them to stick with it, and eventually it happened. Now Ramya has done an off-Broadway play and two films, and just booked her third movie playing the daughter of Janeane Garofalo and David Schwimmer. At this point the Pratts have made more than their investment back, and Ramya's prospects are bright.

I honestly feel that if your child has most of the qualities we discussed in chapter 1, he'll probably have enough success to justify your investment. He may not become the next Haley Joel Osment, but you'll probably make more than your investment back—and have a lot of fun doing it.

Make Yourself Available

Your ability to devote time to your child's career is a key issue— one that can also have a bearing on how much money you spend. Let's say you live close to a major city and your agent wants you to come in for an audition. Your transportation and related expenses are minimal in this case, but you may have to take a day off from work. If you have other young children at home, you may also have to hire a babysitter.

You don't necessarily need lots of money to handle these situations in families where both parents work and can't get away. You can hire a driver to take the child on auditions. That may sound extravagant, but it often costs less than either parent taking time off from work. In many cases a driver doesn't have to cost a lot of money. Instead of using a professional car service, why not recruit a student or a neighbor who would like to make some extra cash for a few hours of work? Of course, you'll want to be sure it's someone you know well or have checked out thoroughly. If your family simply can't afford either time away from work or a driver, you might be able to find an aunt or grandparent to take the child on auditions. There are any number of ways to get the job done, but the point is this: Until your child is old enough to travel on her own, someone has to be there to accompany her from the very beginning of her career.

If your daughter lands a part in a local dinner theater production, are you going to have the time to bring her to the show and take her home every night? If not, who will be available in your place? These are questions that you should be able to answer before the need actually arises.

Once your child's career really starts to take off, the question of availability becomes an even more crucial factor. Your child can be called for a major **screen test** with almost no advance notice. I often get a phone call at four or five in the afternoon asking for a child to be on the plane with his mother early the next morning for a screen test on the West Coast. Every parent starts out with the dream that something like this will happen for her child, but many are unprepared to deal with the suddenness of it all.

Screen test:

An audition that is filmed or videotaped for evaluation purposes.

In the event that your agent calls with this kind of good news, you'd better be ready. Is there an aunt or cousin or grandmother lined up who can manage your household or actually travel with the child if you can't go? Again, you need to have these people lined up beforehand. Don't wait until the last minute. It would be tragic to have an opportunity like this come along only to go down the drain because you weren't available.

I always assume a child is available to audition unless I'm told otherwise. Don't ever disappear. If your family is going on a vacation, let the agent know; otherwise she might schedule auditions for your child while you're away. Vacations with your family are important. On the other hand, if you're planning to go to the Caribbean on a vacation and your child is called to audition for a major motion picture, it's time for a family conference.

I would hope that the child would be available in this situation, but I also understand what a tough choice it can be. I've had many major family vacations and other important events canceled because of sudden **bookings** and auditions. I've also had to ask seventeen-year-olds to make decisions such as, "Do I want to go to my senior prom or do I want to be in a TV commercial?" I'm prepared to accept either decision. My job is to present the pros and the cons of the situation. Ultimately, though, the choice rests with the child and her family.

Booking:

The contracting or engagement of a performer, a production, a theater, or the services of an acting company.

Stay Flexible

If you're the kind of person who has a nervous breakdown when your life isn't in perfect order, you're probably better off not getting involved in the unpredictable world of show business. Mothers who always do their laundry on Monday, the grocery shopping on Tuesday, and the baking on Wednesday are going to have problems. The same is true of fathers who have to have eight hours of sleep and dinner on the table at six o'clock. It's just not going to work for people who fall apart when the unexpected happens, because in this business the unexpected is exactly what you have to expect. Let me give you an example.

One of my clients, Cameron Johann (the boy from the *Oliver!* story earlier), landed a role in a film that was being shot in England. It was on a Friday that I received the initial call from the casting director, who said, "Alert the parents that we may be sending Cameron over for a screen test in London on Tuesday, even though he doesn't definitely have the part yet. Tell them to pack

with two or three months in mind, because if he gets it, we're going to keep him here that long." .

On Monday the casting director called back and said, "It's
not tomorrow, but it may be Wednesday." On Tuesday she said,
"It's definitely tomorrow." Wednesday morning at 10:00 A.M.,
Cameron, his mother, and his baby brother were climbing aboard
a plane to England. Cameron got the part, and the whole family
spent three months abroad.

Situations like this can turn into exciting adventures for the
whole family. But while you're waiting for things to get resolved,
your schedule can be thrown into a frantic and chaotic state. Here
are some things you can do on a day-to-day basis to help minimize the chaos:

- Try to arrange your child's school schedule so that he has only
  nonessential classes at the end of the day. That way, if you
  want to pull him out of school early to attend an audition,
  it won't adversely affect his schoolwork. You can also ask to
  have your child's work assigned in advance when he's going to
  miss classes. If you let the officials at your child's school know
  what you're doing, they will probably be very cooperative.
- Keep your child's clothing in good condition. Make sure
  that he always has an appropriate outfit available and is
  ready to go on an audition on short notice. Don't ever let
  his supply of clothing get down to the bottom of the bar-
  rel. There's nothing worse than having your agent call with
  an audition when you're down to one dirty T-shirt and a
  pair of mud-encrusted sneakers.
- It's also a good policy to send your child to school with
  clean hair. That way, if an audition comes in after he's left
  for school, you are both prepared.

When my children were working professionally, I always had an audition outfit ready to go. If a sudden casting call came for my daughter, for example, I would wet a washcloth, put it in a plastic bag, grab the outfit, and meet her at school. While we were driving, she would wash her face and hands and change her clothes. By the time we arrived at the audition, she looked her best. Remember: You are your child's first manager, so be professional and be prepared to run quickly.

Learn to Roll with the Punches

It's important to understand that show business doesn't work like any other business. It just doesn't behave. I can call and say, "I have an audition for your daughter tomorrow at three." Then at two-thirty I can call and say, "The audition has been canceled." I have no control whatsoever over that kind of sudden change. Sometimes the powers-that-be decide to scrap a project altogether. I've had children in rehearsal for six weeks only to have the show canceled.

Recently I had two children in the new production of *The Miracle Worker* starring Hilary Swank. It tried out at a North Carolina theater and was scheduled to open on Broadway in ten days. The show photos were outside the theater. The set was finished. The costumes were ready. But when I called the producer's office to arrange for opening night tickets, I heard, "Guess what? The decision was made ten minutes ago. There is no opening. *Miracle Worker* isn't going to happen." The actors would be paid two weeks salary, but there would not be one performance on Broadway.

Interestingly, I find that fathers more than mothers have a particularly difficult time understanding unexpected changes. They say, "What do you mean it's not going to happen?" The answer is that even though there's no particular rhyme or reason, it's just not going to happen.

I recall one father who couldn't deal with the cancellation of a commercial that his son was in. The commercial was about to run, but it was scrapped because one of the actors had a contractual conflict. "What do you mean they're not going to use the commercial?" the irate father demanded. Again I had to explain a situation that would probably not occur in most other businesses: "Your child did this commercial and was paid. Normally, it would have run. But when they found out that one of the actors in the commercial had a possible conflict with another product, they decided not to go with it."

People can have a difficult time understanding that in show business, irrational and unpredictable things happen every day as a matter of course. That's why I always stress to parents the importance of rolling with the punches and understanding that there's no rhyme or reason in this business.

I realize how easy it is for parents to feel that their child is being toyed with or that I'm not giving them the whole story when I say, "I don't know." The truth is, sometimes I just don't have the answers and neither does anyone else. But there is one thing I do know for sure: This is a crazy, unpredictable business, so you'd better be prepared for the ball to take some strange bounces.

Get the Whole Family into the Act

For you and your child to make a go of this, you must have the backing of a supportive family unit. If somebody is going to be furious when dinner's not on the table at six because Emily is at an audition, the family's going to crumble very quickly. Everyone in the family has to be behind the decision to let this child try to be a performer. That's why the parents have to value the interests of each child. If Emily's going to audition on Broadway, Dad has to take Jason whitewater rafting or roller-skating or out to play baseball.

When one child becomes the focus of a lot of attention, the other children become resentful. One way to avoid this is to include them as much as possible. If, for instance, Sarah has to come into town for an audition, maybe you can take Jonathan, who loves to see the dinosaurs, to the Museum of Natural History. That way Jonathan won't resent Sarah, because he's getting part of the time, too.

One of my clients, Jimmy Dieffenbach, comes from a family with five children—three of them are interested in performing and two are not. Of the three who are performers, only Jimmy is really successful, having most recently starred as the Pauper in the musical *The Prince and the Pauper* in New York. All the Dieffenbach children are attractive and talented. All could be in the business if they wanted, but some of them choose not to be. They have other interests, including sports. The Dieffenbachs see show business as only one thing their children are involved in. Like most of my successful families, the Dieffenbachs are totally involved with and supportive of the interests of all of their children.

Braden Danner, who was the original Gavroche in *Les Miserables*, Control in *Starlight Express*, and Oliver in *Oliver!* with Patti LuPone, all Broadway productions, as well as a member of *The Mickey Mouse Club*, has just graduated from USC Film School. His older sister, Diane, has never wanted to perform but is an excellent artist. His younger sister, Demaree, who was a baby when Braden started his career, later followed Braden into *Les Miserables* on Broadway and toured the country as Mary in *The Secret Garden* and in *Big, The Musical.* Their mom has been equally supportive of *all* of their career choices.

Donald Faison, who is currently starring as Turk on NBC's

Scrubs, has been a performer since he was a child. His youngest brother, Olamidé, is following in his footsteps, playing Miles on *Sesame Street* and recording as a part of the hit group Imajin for Universal Records. Their middle brother, Dade, is just as successful but has chosen a different path. He was a star basketball player in both prep school and college and is now coaching a high school team.

The parents of all of these young people understand that the activities of their children who don't perform are every bit as important as those of the ones who do. I've had many parents call and say, "Our neighbor is going to bring Sarah in for her audition because we have to go to Jonathan's Little League game." It's that kind of attitude that keeps families of successful young performers together.

Keep a Healthy Perspective on Your Child's Success

Are you the kind of parent who can take disappointment and not make the child feel that he hasn't done well? There's a lot of disappointment and rejection in this business, and it's up to you to keep your child feeling good about himself. When a parent calls me after every audition to ask, "How did Tyler do?" it always sounds as if the parent is more concerned for herself than for the child.

This business can place a lot of pressure on parents. It's very difficult to see your child hurting and sad because he did not land a part. When that happens, there's really no one in particular for you to be mad at—least of all the child. In situations like this it's especially important to keep a healthy perspective. As a rule, if you don't build things up too high, you and your child are not going to fall too far.

There are times when it becomes particularly difficult to maintain your emotional balance. Imagine how you might feel, for example, if your child came in second for a major role. That's one of the toughest situations you can ever come up against.

Sometimes the anguish stretches out for weeks. Your child's agent may make you and your child feel good by saying, "The casting director called to say that you're terrific and one of the top contenders for the role." They may even fly you to L.A., put you up in a fancy hotel, and introduce you to the producers.

As long as they want you, everything's great. But then, if you don't get the part, it's all over in a flash. Suddenly you're on the next plane home, and that's it.

This type of situation can be extremely hard on you, but these are the times when your child needs you the most. For some reason, the closer you come to that elusive brass ring, the more painful it is to lose out. If this happens two or three times and you take it as a personal rejection, it can become emotionally devastating for the child.

The key to handling such setbacks is to turn the whole thing into a positive experience, not a do-or-die situation. It's much better to tell the child, "Look how close you came. Three hundred children were auditioning for this part and you were one of the final two considered. Think about what that says about your talent and your chances of landing the next part." Remember, your child will take his cue from you. If you can handle the rejection and keep it in perspective, so will he.

While we're on the subject of rejection, I'd like to offer another piece of advice that can help you and your child maintain a healthy perspective. For the most part it's best not to talk about things until they materialize. If Tyler has an audition for a big Disney movie, don't tell your neighbors and friends about it. If you do and Tyler doesn't get the part, he'll have to live through the disappointment all over again. Everyone will say, "So, you didn't get it, huh? What happened?" Even if you're down to the final two, it's best not to talk about it. Of course, if he does get the part, it's okay to tell everybody and make a fuss. But to talk about it and then make the child live through the horror of saying, "I didn't get it" over and over is like reliving the same nightmare twelve or fourteen times.

Also, people can get pretty bored listening to you brag. Your neighbors don't want to hear that Tyler was in this magazine or in that TV commercial any more than you want to see the same pictures of their summer vacation over and over again. You may be excited that your child is on TV, but your neighbors will get tired of it in a hurry. It's far better to let people tell you that they saw your child on a TV commercial than for you to tell them.

I realize that many parents find it hard not to boast. Still, if you talk about these things all the time, your child is going to do the same. That kind of bragging will only bring a lot of resentment from the other kids. Most of my successful clients shy away from discussing show business, unless someone else brings the subject up first. If your child takes that kind of approach, instead of trying to impress everybody with his stardom, he is more likely to keep in good standing with his friends. As a parent, you can help your child stay well adjusted by not thinking and talking about show business constantly.

Another key emotional area in which a child needs your help is in dealing with the competition. How does Sarah relate to that other little girl who looks just like her and could just as well get the part? The answer depends greatly on your attitude. I feel that it's very important for these kids to know and respect one another. They need to understand that negative feelings toward their competition won't help them do better. After all, they're in this together.

It is not at all unusual for people in show business to become friends with their closest competitors. "Once you get to know your competitors," I tell my young clients, "you may find out that their personalities and interests are a lot like yours. That's probably one important reason why you're such close competitors."

You can help your child a great deal by conveying a healthy attitude about competition. But like many sensitive emotional issues, it's difficult to convey something positive when our own attitudes need some reshaping. Adults should have more control over their actions than children. Nevertheless, I have seen too many talented boys and girls never reach their potential because their parents were misguided. I hope this chapter has helped you consider your feelings and attitudes in a clearer light.

How You Can Help Your Child Succeed—NOTES

- Evaluate your child's potential realistically.
- Be a supportive parent; let your child set the pace.
- Work within your budget.
- Make this a positive experience for the whole family.
- Be prepared for the unexpected.
- Help your child stay well adjusted by not thinking and talking about show business constantly.

3

Building a Strong Foundation

Now that we've talked about the qualities that both you and your child need to make this work, I'd like to show you how to help your child build a solid foundation—the kind that will support him as he moves ahead in his career. A young person may have all the talent in the world, but unless that talent is developed correctly with proper training and strengthened through a series of even more challenging proving grounds, it may go totally unrecognized and unrewarded.

Training

Many children take singing and dance lessons with no thought of a professional career. If your child is looking for a hobby, you probably don't have to be all that particular about training. If the teacher is at all competent and your child seems to be enjoying the classes, that's generally reason enough to continue. When a child does want to work professionally, however, a parent should be far more selective. It's important for aspiring performers to find the right training as early as possible. In most communities there are any number of teachers and schools offering lessons. Here are some guidelines to help you make the best choices.

Singers

Many children are wonderful natural singers, but there are very few who can sing correctly without training. I recently met a six-year-old girl who, although she never had a lesson, sang properly. I'm told that the late Ethel Merman had that same gift. But these are two very rare exceptions to the rule. More often, I see the inexperienced child with a good ear and nice pitch who becomes strained and red in the face when she tries to project her voice and reach high notes.

There is a common misconception that children shouldn't study voice. This is absolutely wrong. If a child is hoping to perform eight shows a week on Broadway, she'd better be singing correctly and keeping her voice healthy.

I can always tell when young singers are straining and hurting their voices. They get red in the face, and you can see tightness in the neck muscles. If your child's voice is hoarse or his throat gets sore when he sings a lot, these are other signs that he may not be singing correctly. Remember, a child who sings improperly can damage his vocal cords and permanently jeopardize a promising career.

---

*"It's very hard to find a good **voice teacher**," says Richard Barrett, a well-respected New York vocal instructor who works with children as well as adults. "Unlike a doctor, for instance, who has to be licensed, anyone can*

say they're a voice teacher. The general rule is that if the child is studying with someone and something doesn't feel right in his throat, he should talk to his parent about it right away, and the parent should begin to look for a different voice teacher. A person only has one set of vocal chords for a lifetime. It's not like when you break a guitar string and you can replace it with a new one.

"In starting your search for a voice teacher," Barrett continues, "look for a person who has the patience to work with children. One of the most difficult things in training children is their short attention span. You have to teach them how to concentrate without discouraging them. You have to find a balance that keeps the animation and excitement and still helps them to settle down to learn. I find a half-hour to forty-five minutes for a lesson long enough in the beginning."

Voice teacher:

A professional whose focus is building the instrument by teaching proper vocal technique, posture, and breathing.

Young singers—especially those with outstanding natural voices—should begin studying with a qualified voice teacher as early as possible, to find out what they're doing right and wrong. Some voice teachers really don't offer appropriate training for aspiring professionals or are unwilling to train a young voice because they are unsure of how to do it properly. They teach their students lots of songs, but not the technique required for working situations. But a good teacher approaches voice training from the point of view of building a sensitive instrument. I've had dozens of clients perform on Broadway, and not one child who had been trained properly experienced any lasting vocal problems.

*"Everyone who teaches children to sing correctly is in agreement on certain things," says Robert Marks, a well-known New York **vocal coach**. "Jaw tension, closed mouth, and attempting to sing too high or too low are all signs of a voice that needs training.*

"When you go to a voice teacher, the main thing you're buying is a different set of ears. That's why people who sing at the Met still study—because it's so hard to be objective about your own voice. The problem with many young singers is that they've been to a vocal coach without first going to a voice teacher."

Vocal coach:

A professional accompanist and arranger. He helps a performer choose songs, transpose them into the right key, and prepare to perform them.

A vocal coach is usually a fine accompanist who can put anything in any key. He also may be a fine arranger who can help a young singer select and perform dynamite songs. But a voice teacher is, essentially, a person whose focus is building the instrument and getting rid of interference and tension. When I evaluate a singer, I use two yardsticks: listening to the voice and observing what a person is doing. If a person's eyebrows are going up, that's an obvious indication of some tension somewhere in the system. In teaching proper vocal technique, we're dealing with the coordination of all the parts. If the posture is good, it will permit the breathing mechanism to function a lot better. If that's working well, then the throat can be opened more easily. Good singing is the by-product of an open throat in coordination with breath support. All of these things should be happening without strain if you've been trained properly.

*"Warm-ups are an essential part of every lesson and performance," says Marks. "These are scales and exercises done **in head** or soprano voice to exercise and strengthen the vocal cords. A good voice teacher will give you a series of warm-ups to use each time you begin a lesson or perform publicly."*

In-head voice:

A lighter, breathier voice, as compared to the deeper, normal voice, which is sustained by the diaphragm, a muscle below the rib cage.

It's not all that difficult to find a good teacher, but you may have to do some research. You might try calling a university in your area and asking if there's an artist-in-residence in their voice department. Local agents and managers are other good sources for referrals for qualified teachers who work extensively with young people.

"There are two kinds of singing—good singing and bad singing," Richard Barrett explains. "It's the voice teacher's job to teach the child to sing well. He does that through the songs as well as through technique and exercises. He should teach the child how to take care of her voice, too, from a health point of view—how to sing around it when she is sick. Pop music has given everyone the idea that singing is easier than acting or dancing when, in fact, it's more difficult because you can't see your vocal chords when you're singing. It's all a big mystery, really."

In selecting a voice teacher for your child, look for someone who is sensitive to the kinds of physical and psychological changes young people have to endure. One of the most trying ordeals—especially for boys—is when the voice begins to change.

When a young male singer's voice starts to change, someone else in the ensemble will invariably say, "Oh, your voice is sounding lower today." This is a not very subtle way of telling him that in a few months he's going to be replaced by a younger singer. This can be a real tragedy for some kids. I try to help my clients deal with this trauma by pointing them ahead to new and better things. Richard Barrett has some thoughts on this difficult transition.

"It takes a long time to learn how to sing correctly, and the job never ends. Every seven years the body goes through a metabolic change, and when that happens, the voice changes, too. So adjustments have to be made. The most dramatic change for a boy happens at puberty at about thirteen or fourteen. It can be very scary for a boy, and he needs to be reassured that if he keeps vocalizing and training, his new sound will emerge and fill out. It takes a good year, really, to get used to that new voice. He may even go through a time when his pitch is not so good because he's unaccustomed to the sound coming out of his mouth. I don't do elaborate scales at that point—maybe only three or four tone scales—until he hears the pitch again.

"Girls go through a less obvious change. Much of that involves controlling the air flow through their vocal chords. Seventh- and eighth-grade girls begin to sound like vacuum cleaners because they have too much air escaping with their notes. The big change for women, however, comes around their thirtieth birthday. A high lyric soprano will get a darker, richer tone and lose some of those really high notes. It's most important for women to develop a sound technique between the ages of fifteen and twenty-five. Otherwise, when they get into that big change in their thirties they'll be unprepared to handle it."

With so much hanging in the balance in terms of both your child's career and his emotional health, don't look at voice lessons as a place to cut corners. If the best teacher in your area wants to charge a somewhat higher price, it's probably well worth the extra expense. Bad lessons can damage your child's voice for a long time—possibly forever.

If I were interviewing a voice teacher for my son or daughter, I would ask a lot of questions. I would find out what sort of people he works with and what kind of product he is interested in turning out. I would also ask what he is specifically looking for in a student and measure that against what you are specifically looking for in a voice teacher.

Every teacher has a different approach. For example, some teachers don't have beginning students practice, because what are they going to practice—the same wrong note ten times? Instead, they have them listen to a tape of their most recent lesson every day. After a while they start to hear how they are supposed to sing, and that becomes an automatic response.

Once a child starts to study, a parent who attends the lessons often finds that his or her own ears start to improve. This kind of exposure can help you evaluate whether or not your child is receiving the right kind of training. If all is going well, you should start noticing that the sound of the child's voice is getting fuller and more beautiful. It's also important to make sure that your child's range is increasing in both directions. With proper vocal training you should find that things that were difficult for your child to sing a month ago are now a lot easier.

Dancers

Good training early in the game is equally as important for dancers as it is for singers. To find good dance training try to contact professional dancers and ask them where they studied. You might also call local universities and talent agencies for referrals. When you interview dance instructors, ask if they've worked professionally. Find out if they were trained in New York and if they periodically return to New York to take classes and maintain their contacts. Perhaps most important, you should ask prospective teachers whether any of their students are dancing professionally in one of the major show business centers.

"If I had a choice between a teacher who had decided to start a dance school after touring with a company or performing as a Radio City Rockette, and one who started teaching right out of college," advises Frank Hatchett, one of the founders of the Broadway Dance Center in New York and a nationally known jazz instructor, "I would certainly pick the one with prior professional experience. She's gone back home after working but still loves to dance. I would also look for a teacher who continues to study in the city. She takes the time to get her juices going and keeps current with what's going on. There is a difference between a kid being taught or just taking class. In other words, is the teacher just giving class, or is she teaching class?"

Please don't be afraid to ask questions, and don't be intimidated. Ask if you can watch some classes to see how the children dance.

But remember: Fancy recitals, competition trophies, and cute costumes are not what professional dancing is all about. That's why the teacher who puts on the best dance recital may not necessarily offer the best training.

"You should look for a school that spends the entire first half of the teaching year on technique," says Frank Hatchett. "The focus should be on cleaning up

the dancer technically—the control, the turns, the beats—and then in the spring semester they should begin to work on **choreography,** *which would evolve into competition dancing or a recital at the end of the school year. There is a whole new breed of dancer today because of competitions. When I judge them I give comments on each child. When the student goes back home after the competition, it's up to the teacher to work on cleaning up those things. So often, when I go back the next year, the dancer is still making the same mistake he made the year before. Competitions have to be treated as learning experiences, not just a way to earn a trophy at the end."*

Choreography:
The art of creating and arranging dances or ballets.

It's worth taking the time to find the right dance teacher. When you start visiting dance schools, you may be surprised to find that the flashiest school isn't necessarily the one that offers the best training. When too much time is spent on flash, sometimes not enough time is spent learning the solid basics that one needs to work as a professional dancer.

"Find out what the style of the school is," Hatchett urges. "Are they lyrical, hip-hop, funky, or just classical? Can the child experience a variety of styles in the school? A school that brings in guest instructors who are working dancers or big-city teachers often has the most to offer. Make sure the school groups their classes by ability, not just by age.

"Encourage a child to take a ballet class to become aware of her body and get her center. Ballet can be a turnoff for some kids, especially boys. If you have a boy who wants to dance, look for a school that is sensitive to teaching the male dancer. I cringe to think of how many wonderful male dancers

we lost or never got to see because of the wrong teacher. A lot of times teachers forget that there are boys in the class. If a boy has a dream to dance, it can be lost by a teacher making that kind of mistake.

"I had a group of black boys when I began teaching in Springfield, Massachusetts. I used to put on music by James Brown, who was very popular at the time. I would say, 'Bend the knees, now go up on the bar, now feet down,'" Hatchett continues with a chuckle. "Later they found out that they were doing demi-pliés and relevés. I told them, 'Okay, we're going to a convention and you're going to take a ballet class as well as a jazz class. They have a male teacher, and it will be good for you.' I said, 'I'm going to be watching you and I dare you to leave the class early.'

"Well, we got to the class and there were about a hundred little girls, two white boys, and my twelve black boys. The teacher came in and said, 'This is so great. Today we're going to be fairies, so get up on your tippy, tippy toes.' My guys looked at me, and I gave them a nod. Those boys did the best grand jetés out the door so fast. I took them into the stairwell outside and said, 'Okay, I was wrong about this.' I almost lost some of those kids over that.

"I saw the teacher later and said, 'How could you not see those twelve African-American boys? Why didn't you just say, 'We're going to do "The Dance of the Sugar Plum Fairy" today, and I have a special part for you men'?

"When I do workshops on the weekends, I always include a teacher session as well. At that session, I include a section on how to teach little boys."

One of the ways I can spot a good teacher is by how well her students do professionally. When I see several students of a particular local teacher end up in New York working on Broadway, I know that teacher is good. I once met a great teacher in Kentucky who runs a little school out of the basement of her home. I couldn't believe some of the things her students were able to do. There's another teacher in Ohio who currently has more than a dozen former students working professionally in New York. There are any number of wonderful local teachers whose students go on to work in major professional situations. That kind of success rate is probably due to the difference between fair training and solid, professional instruction.

As with singing, it's better not to have any dance training than to have the wrong training, so don't be penny-wise and pound-foolish. Actually, dance classes are not very expensive. And surprisingly, they are often much cheaper in New York than in suburban areas. Dancers in New York can buy a ten-lesson card for $130—only $13 a lesson. That's one important reason many parents of aspiring professional dancers find it a good investment to spend a summer in the New York area.

Actors

As far as I'm concerned, training for a young actor is far less important than natural talent and experience. In fact, training can sometimes cause more harm than good. The real training comes from doing. My main advice to young actors is to act as much as possible—whether in school plays or local theater productions.

In general, I would rather not see a child have any acting training at first. Successful child actors seem to have a natural feel for role-playing. Some children are born with that ability, just as some musically gifted children are born with perfect pitch.

No matter how much natural talent a child has, technique will become more important as he matures. That's where training comes in. Some actors who are successful when they're young can't seem to cross over from acting naturally to acting with the kind of technique an adult professional needs. Any child who is serious about acting as a career eventually will require training to develop the necessary technique.

Here's how I see the progression for young actors: first they need talent, then experience, and then training. Children who receive acting training too soon can become artificial and self-conscious. They can lose that natural quality that is so important in film and television work.

Shakespearean actors are not what we want for film and TV. As a matter of fact, an overcoached child is exactly what we *don't* want. We want a child who is relaxed and natural enough to pretend that he's someone else. That's why I encourage aspiring young actors to join local groups that put on plays with lots of **improvisation.**

Improvisation:

A spontaneous performance done on the spur of the moment, without any specific preparation.

I should mention that the training requirements for commercials are much different from those for film and theater. "Most children need very little preparation to do commercials," says my daughter, Bonnie Deroski, who is the head of our agency's commercial department. She adds:

"What commercial clients are looking for is the natural personality of the child. I think learning basic commercial technique, such as how to work in front of a camera, how to avoid the temptation to look at the video monitor, and understanding how to read a commercial script and use a cue card, can be helpful. For the slow warmer, a commercial class can help him perform in a less self-conscious way. And for the child who has had a lot of stage experience, an on-camera class can ease her out of the habit of projecting to

the back of the house and get her used to scaling her acting down to the small screen."

Handling commercial copy is a very specific kind of acting skill—one that can be taught in a relatively short time. Children who want to work in commercials usually find commercial acting classes beneficial. These classes are often listed in trade publications.

Hobbies—It Pays to Play

Any activity that your child does just for fun may be the deciding factor that lands him a job. This is particularly true in commercials. I've had requests for soccer players, gymnasts, skateboarders, violin players, jugglers, dirt bikers, magicians, and almost anything else you can think of that children do for fun.

The very first commercial I ever booked as an agent was a Dr Pepper commercial with a roller skater in it. I received a phone call from a casting director for a new Dr Pepper advertising campaign. She was looking for a twelve-year-old boy who was a dynamite roller skater. I had only been an agent for about six weeks, and I couldn't find a great roller skater who was that age. However, I did know a former roller-skating champion named Scott Ross. He was twenty years old but looked quite a bit younger.

Though I was a relative rookie, I was bold enough to call the casting director back and ask, "Would you consider someone who is older but who has a young look and skates great?" She said, "Sure. Why don't you send him over?" Scott landed the job and was seen roller-skating on the same Dr Pepper commercial that featured Fred Flintstone and Jimmie "JJ" Walker.

More recently, a client of mine, Stephen Walker Hund, landed an ongoing role on the soap opera *One Life to Live* because he played the drums. They were putting together a backup band for the teen singer on the show and needed actors with a working knowledge of instruments. When Stephen auditioned for the part, he was able to demonstrate his drumming ability for the show's producers. Stephen is a fine actor, but I know he landed that part because he's an excellent drummer as well.

Almost any hobby a child has can, at some point, give him that extra edge. Not too long ago we needed a mountain climber for a cereal commercial. We called around and found out that one of our clients was a skilled mountain climber. Before he was hired, he was flown to Hawaii and asked to prove that he was indeed capable of climbing a mountain. He spent a week in Hawaii shooting that commercial (a pretty nice fringe benefit). Mountain climbing wasn't a skill that this person had ever used before as an actor. It was just one of his hobbies, but it landed him a job.

My agency receives all sorts of requests for children with special skills. Sometimes we're asked for girls who are experienced cheerleaders or boys who skateboard well. Athletic skills are also useful, as are instrumental and vocal skills. Not long ago the Broadway production of the opera *La Bohème* needed children who not only sang extremely well, but also roller-skated. They went so far as to take the children who had made it through the vocal auditions to a roller rink to test their skating skills. So you never know what hobby will one day help your child land a job.

As we saw in chapter 1, well-rounded children often succeed as performers. That doesn't mean that you should start pushing your child to pursue different hobbies. On the other hand, I would encourage a child to be as well-rounded as possible. Not only are these non-show-business activities good for the child's personal development, they can also pay off in terms of landing more jobs.

Proving Grounds

Although some children break into this business on a high level without any previous experience, most have to start out small and build gradually. Here are some suggestions for helping your child take those important initial steps toward a successful professional career.

School Plays

These are great initial proving grounds and enjoyable experiences for most children. I encourage children to participate in as many school productions as possible. They have fun with their friends and they learn something about group participation. If a child doesn't get a role in the school play, however, it has no bearing on my judgment of his ability to act professionally. I've represented many children who have had positive initial performing experiences in school productions. But I've also met talented young actors who, for one reason or another, didn't participate in their school plays. Some children have scheduling difficulties, while others have problems with their teachers. I've seen children have their lives made miserable by drama teachers who were envious of their students' talents. A supportive high school drama teacher, on the other hand, can be just wonderful. I'm happy to say that most of the high school drama teachers I meet are very supportive of talented children. But be aware that you can encounter the other kind.

Once your child starts working professionally, he may not have time to participate in school plays, which tend to have very demanding rehearsal schedules. Directors of school plays often are not very flexible when it comes to letting children miss rehearsals. They realize that most of the young participants need a great deal of preparation and they are not about to bend the rules for one or two exceptional children.

School plays may require three or four months of rehearsal for two nights of performance; that's not the way it is in professional theater. Even most major Broadway shows rehearse for no more than five or six weeks. If your child is ready to tackle more challenging proving grounds, he may well have to drop out of future school productions.

Community and University Theaters

These are the best and most logical proving grounds after school plays. Community theaters are groups of local people who put on plays basically for fun. They charge admission to cover their production costs, and generally, nobody gets paid. To find such theater groups in your area, look for newspaper advertisements or posters in the windows of local stores announcing a new show. Call the people who are producing the show and ask if the production has any roles for children. Normally, community groups don't have children participating on a regular basis. Therefore, if a child is needed for a particular part, he or she will often be cast through an open audition.

Another good place for your child to get started is with a local university theater. If the play being produced calls for a child, the logical place to look is in the community. Contact the school's drama department to find out if there is a way for your child to become involved in one of their upcoming productions. Let them know that your child is interested in any appropriate roles that are available, and ask them to contact you when auditions are held.

Local Dinner Theaters

Usually these are profit-making ventures and often there is some pay involved. For this reason they are more challenging and meaningful proving grounds than either community or university productions. Many of the children I represent experienced their first taste of professional acting in dinner theater productions. These theaters operate all over the country, and they are great places to get started.

Dinner theaters frequently hold **open calls** when they need children for their productions. If shows such as *Annie* or *The Sound of Music* or *Oliver!* or *The Music Man* are being produced by a dinner theater in your area, try to put yourself on their telephone or mailing list so that they'll call you when they hold auditions. Sometimes your child can have a chance to work with established actors and respected directors. Those well-known names will look great on her **résumé** next to the **credit** for the show.

Open call:

An audition that is open to the general public.

Résumé:

A listing of the performer's physical statistics, union affiliations, training, hobbies, and credits.

Credit:

A list of performing experiences included on a resume.

Dinner and regional theater productions provide great opportunities for your child to get her feet wet. They are also terrific proving grounds in a number of important ways. Working in local productions gives a child a chance to see if performing is something she really likes and wants to do. These productions demand a great deal of a child's time—far more time than some talented children are willing to devote. Also, a child's success on the local level is usually a good indication of her potential. If your child can't get a part in a local dinner theater or community theater production, she's probably not going to be able to work professionally.

Dinner Theater:

A type of professional theater at which dinner is served before the performance, the cost of which is included in the ticket price.

Regional Theater:

A major professional theater doing full-scale productions outside New York and Los Angeles.

National Touring Companies

National touring companies of Broadway shows offer one of the most exciting opportunities for children trying to break into the business. Producers and casting directors frequently conduct auditions for understudies, replacements, and guest actors when their productions are booked into cities around the country. Casting notices for these auditions can be found in your local newspaper and often on local television news programs.

Many of the children discovered at these local auditions—from cities as varied as Honolulu and Detroit—have ended up performing on Broadway. These auditions can give your child his big break—without ever leaving his hometown.

Local TV

If the résumés I receive from young performers around the country are any indication, there is plenty of work on local and cable TV. Videotapes of your child performing on a local program or commercial are valuable tools when you are trying to interest agents in major markets. If you do have videotape from a professional job that your child worked on locally, be sure to note on his résumé, "Tape available."

To find opportunities on local television, call all the broadcast and cable stations in your area and ask if they ever have a need for children. In larger cities talent is usually handled through agents. But in smaller markets the direct approach can pay off. Once again, don't be afraid to ask for information; the worst they can do is say no. The opportunities in local television are out there. I strongly urge you to pursue them.

Working on the local level—whether in theater or TV— gives a child the kind of foundation he needs to move ahead in this business. These experiences are valuable proving grounds for you, as well as for your child. During the time that your son or daughter is working locally, you'll have the chance to evaluate your ability and willingness to deal with the demands of being a show business parent. Can you handle the emotional stress? Can you devote the time needed to drive your child to and from auditions, rehearsals, and performances without neglecting the rest of the family? These are important questions that you need to answer before attempting to take your child's career to the next step.

Building a Strong Foundation—NOTES

- Seek out appropriate training and local work to help your child gain valuable experience.
- A voice teacher is a person whose focus is building the instrument. She teaches proper vocal technique, posture, and breathing.
- A vocal coach is an accompanist and an arranger. He helps a performer choose songs, transpose them into the right key, and prepare to perform them.
- A good dance teacher has worked professionally, continues to train in New York (or other major cities), and has students who go on to work professionally.
- Don't look for the flashiest dance school and the fanciest recitals. Dancers should learn the basic vocabulary and rudiments of dance. At a professional audition dancers must be prepared to listen to a choreographer and learn the combinations quickly.
- Young actors first need talent, then experience, then training. Professional and amateur theaters often advertise open auditions in local newspapers.

4

Moving Ahead

One of the questions I'm most often asked by parents is, "How do I know when it's time to move from the local level to a major market?" I really believe that if you've gone through all the steps we've discussed in the first three chapters, you'll know when the time is right. And if for some reason you don't figure it out, someone else will probably tell you that your child is ready to move on.

Several years before I became an agent, my daughter, Bonnie, was working in a local New Jersey community theater production. One day Mark LaMura, the director of that show, came to me and said, "Your daughter is too good to be working locally. It's time for you to look for a New York agent who can send her on major auditions." Frankly, I was skeptical at first. But this director convinced me to give it a try. He asked a friend of his to shoot a roll of pictures. We selected the best one and had some prints made up. Then he showed me how to write a résumé. At that point he personally introduced Bonnie to a New York agent.

Within a short time she booked several roles in feature films and an **off-Broadway** show.

<u>Off-Broadway:</u>
A group of New York City theaters that produce Broadway-type shows on a smaller, less expensive scale.

If your child really has the talent, people are going to recognize it, especially professionals who work with her on the local level. If nobody has approached you, though, and you are uncertain whether it's time to start thinking about moving ahead, it's perfectly appropriate to bluntly ask someone whose opinion you respect: "Do you think my child is ready to move beyond the local level?" Your child's teacher, the director of the community theater group, or a local agent is often a good person to approach for this kind of feedback.

When a child goes through the various proving grounds and the response is positive on every level, the time is often right to start tackling greater challenges. But no matter where your child is in his career, it's a good idea to understand well in advance what is involved in pursuing work in major markets. Parents who are aware of the total picture are better able to make intelligent decisions from the start. Remember this: if your child has what it takes, there will come a time when he's done all he can do locally. When that time comes, these are the things you will need to do to help him move ahead.

Take the Right Picture

A good picture is an essential tool in this business. As we've seen, a winning look is very important, and the picture you send to agents must convey that quality. The ideal photograph to send an agent is a straightforward, facing-the-camera shot that really looks like your son or daughter; in other words, a good, representative picture. There shouldn't be any surprises when the child arrives at an agent's office. Please don't send me a shot from three Christmases ago of Michael sitting on Santa Claus's lap, then walk into my office with a totally different boy.

Parents are often unhappy with their child's professional picture. They will say, "Oh, but you can see her crooked teeth," or "Can't we have that mark taken off her face?" The answer is no: I don't have flaws removed because I want the picture to look exactly like the child. If a child has a little darkness around the eyes from a lack of sleep, we might remove that. But generally, we use a true likeness of the child, flaws and all.

Many parents think that their child needs expensive professional photographs to get started. That's just not the case. If your child has the right look, all you need to send to prospective agents and **managers** is an ordinary snapshot. I've received school pictures, Polaroids, and snapshots—all of which are just fine to introduce your child to me. It's this simple: Buy a roll of film, take your child's picture, and select the best one. Then have your local one-hour photo shop make reproductions and send them off to agents and managers.

Manager:
A professional who advises and counsels a performer for a commission. Such professionals may solicit agents for their clients but may not directly solicit union work or negotiate union contracts.

If a photographer tries to talk you into an expensive portfolio, don't listen. No matter what anyone tells you, it doesn't take a $1,000 portfolio or expensive color 5×7s or 8×10s to get started. And remember, you don't need professional photographs until after you've found an agent or a manager. At that point your representative will guide you in selecting the shot that suits his needs.

Even after a child signs with my agency, we rarely require more than one good full-face 8 × 10 picture. Except in rare cases, I just don't need full-body shots of a child swimming or riding a horse or in dance clothing. Sometimes a child who wears glasses may need two pictures, one with the glasses and one without. The total cost of this shouldn't run you much more than $500. That breaks down to around $200–350 for the sitting and perhaps another $140 for 100 reproductions.

Professional pictures come in a wide range of prices. I send most of my newcomers to someone who does a pretty good job and charges $300. On the other hand, I will sometimes suggest another photographer whose prices start at $600 and who does beautiful, top-of-the-line work. He spends about four hours, works digitally, and takes about 200 shots to show the child in a variety of hairstyles and outfits. His lighting is great and he uses very fine lenses on his camera. His finished work is completely re-touched. If there's a little hair hanging over the face, for example, he'll touch that out. The result is absolutely beautiful, clean, highest-quality work.

For most people who are starting to audition professionally, though, my $300 guy is fine. He may spend an hour or so and take about 60 or 70 shots, showing several outfits and hairstyles. He's good with children and very cooperative. In fact, once or twice I've sent him someone who's really had no money, and he's done the session for next to nothing.

I'll only recommend a more expensive photographer when children have progressed sufficiently in their careers to justify that kind of expense. When, for example, an actor has done several major projects and her picture is going to appear in magazines or newspapers, the photo becomes more than just a marketing tool. But unless your child has reached that level or you have an unlimited budget, spending $500 for a photographer just doesn't make sense.

When an adult is trying to break into the business, I generally advise spending as much as he or she can. But children are different. I've seen many promising children decide that they really don't want to be performers after just a few auditions. Still, if money is not a consideration and you want the best, there's no reason not to use a top photographer.

When money is really a problem, you can ask a friend to shoot a roll of film or some digital shots and make 8 × 10s. If you follow my guidelines for wardrobe and photo style, this approach can work just fine. I've also had school pictures reproduced and have used them successfully. I'll sometimes ask a parent with an extremely limited budget, "Do you have last year's school picture? Is it good? Is the contrast sharp enough to copy?"

Whatever your budget, though, please don't make the mistake of sending elaborate pictures to agents and managers. Nothing comes across as more amateurish than a first communion picture or a shot of a child in stage makeup and her dance recital outfit. Please believe me when I say that people in the business are looking for one thing above all in a photograph: *an exact likeness of the child.* Ideally, I'm looking for a good, straightforward, looking-into-the-camera picture that captures not only the look but also the personality of the child.

Since the main purpose of a photograph is to convey a winning look, it's important to pay attention to things like clothes and hair beforehand. Naturally, these factors will become even more important once your child starts auditioning for agents and casting directors. Here, then, are some basic guidelines for you to follow.

Clothes

In selecting an outfit for your child's photograph, keep it simple. A shirt and a sweater or a polo shirt usually work well for boys. Girls can wear a simple shirt, either with or without a sweater or jacket. To avoid having your child's photograph come out looking like he has no neck, steer clear of turtlenecks. Also, stay away from clothes with fancy prints, because these designs sometimes detract from a child's look. Remember, we're trying to draw attention to the child, not his clothes.

When your child goes out to meet agents, he should wear nice, neat, casual clothes—the same sort of thing he'd wear to school. Those casual clothes will also do just fine once an agent starts sending him out on auditions. Directors and casting people usually want children to look and act naturally. New or fancy clothes can make a child uncomfortable. That's why the child's familiar, everyday clothes are usually your best bet.

I can think of only a few instances when I had to ask children to dress up for auditions. When he was seeing children for the musical *A Little Princess,* the casting director requested that the little girls come in dresses because that's the look the play called for. But normally, children should wear what I call good school clothes: jeans and T-shirts and cute sport clothes are among the appropriate choices.

Select bright colors that highlight your child's coloring, but nothing too slick or trendy. Normally, you should go for a look that is very all-American. You have to remember that for the most part, it is the adult audience that we're selling to. Therefore, it's their tastes that have to be addressed.

It's important to select clothes that will stay in style for a number of years—that's why the all-American look works. A lot of films and commercials are produced to be shown, hopefully, for years to come. Therefore, you should try to avoid anything that reeks too much of this year's look.

Hair

As with clothes, it is far better to go with a hairstyle that will not be out of fashion in the near future. Lately I find myself discouraging girls from wearing stylized haircuts. If a girl insists on doing something trendy, I'll tell her to put on a headband or use clips so that she'll have an alternate, less dated hairstyle to wear on auditions.

No matter what the style, though, a child's hair should always be neat. Parents are often surprised when they see their child's picture and find that what they thought was well-groomed hair looks messy. Because these pictures are so close and critical, you can see every hair that's out of place. That's why you have to be very careful that your child's hair is perfect—even to the point of standing nearby with a comb while the photographs are being taken.

As a rule, stick to a simple hairstyle and avoid things like fancy ribbons and bows. Also, don't get your child's hair cut right before the pictures are taken, because it will be quite obvious. Your child will look much more real and natural if he has a haircut a week or two before the photo session. In general, we like children to get their hair trimmed regularly but to avoid drastic haircuts that would alter their looks dramatically.

A child with the flexibility of more than one look will usually have an advantage in this business. If a little girl with long hair can wear it several different ways, you might photograph her first with her hair down, then braid it and have more shots taken. With little boys you might start with very neatly parted and combed hair. Then you might have him change his shirt and mess his hair up to make him look as if he just came in from playing.

In general, casting directors want boys who look like boys and girls who look like girls. That's why most little girls who work have long hair, while little boys generally wear their hair fairly short. Some boys have curly hair that's worn longer because that is often a cute, appealing look. But generally, you won't see too much of the androgynous look.

Create a Look That Sells

If you want to maximize you child's chances in this business, you have to be aware of the kind of look you are trying to create. As we saw in chapter 1, there is a demand for many physical types, but a child must clearly fit into a given category. A chubby child can do very well, as long as he's clearly chubby. On the other hand, when a child who is not supposed to be chubby starts putting on weight, we might have to suggest that she cut out junk food.

What sells and what doesn't sell in the business doesn't necessarily have anything to do with what you see in the real world. For example, many teenagers have acne. But you'll never see a child with acne on TV, not even on pimple cream commercials. Why? Simply because pimples don't sell.

Similarly, braces rarely sell, though there are ways of getting around the braces look. Sometimes you can get removable braces or a set that is worn just at night. There are also clear braces, which generally can't be used on camera, but do work on stage because live audiences can't spot them. I represent some children who have new types of braces that are put on the back of the teeth. They are more expensive and the straightening process takes a little longer, but they're totally invisible.

Glasses, you may be surprised to learn, definitely *do* sell. In fact, there are several saleable looks with glasses. An offbeat child with glasses is a look that sells, as is a very smart child with glasses. And remember: you can have a look that sells with glasses even if you don't really wear glasses. If I sense that creating an intelligent or bookwormy look will help someone work, I'll ask him to buy a pair of glasses with clear lenses.

When you watch TV or go to the movies, try to pick out the different character stereotypes. There's the handsome macho boy, the jock, the smart boy with glasses, the chubby boy, the offbeat boy with jug-handle ears and buckteeth, and the boy who starts out as a nerd and ends up a non-nerd by taking off his glasses and putting himself together in a kind of Clark Kent-to-Superman metamorphosis. Similarly, there's the cute, outgoing girl who always gets the boy; the quiet, beautiful girl; and a variety of girl character types. They can be chubby with glasses, covered with freckles, or offbeat-looking with buckteeth and pigtails.

People in show business are very aware of type differentiation, so it's important that you think in similar terms when you try to help your child create his or her look. There are times when a call comes in for a specific physical type, and there really isn't anything you can do if your child isn't that type. But there are other times when the producers of a show or commercial aren't quite so set on what they're looking for. They may have something in mind, but often they are waiting for a special child to walk in and breathe life into a role.

Write an Appropriate Résumé

The requirements for a good résumé vary from business to business. In some fields it may be desirable to have a lengthy or decorative résumé. Show business is not one of those fields. In our industry, résumés that are decorated with funny little drawings and the like are more likely to bring a laugh than anything else.

Please don't waste your time trying to come up with something elaborate. You'll have better results if you follow the basic format that most professional actors use.

The sample résumé in the Appendix is indicative of our agency's standard form. While you don't have to feel absolutely locked into this format, you should try to stay pretty close. We usually staple the four corners of an actor's résumé to the back of the 8×10 photo. Therefore, the information on a résumé must be limited to one page.

The child's name should appear on top. Right under that you list any union affiliations. Vital statistics are often listed on the right side of the page. These include height, weight, hair color, eye color, the age range a child can realistically play, and date of birth. If you have an agent, put her name, address, and phone number on the left side of the page.

For your child's protection I suggest that you don't include your home address and phone number on the résumé. You never know who is going to get their hands on the pictures you send out. Many actors subscribe to voice mail services or have pager numbers for that purpose. If people in the business want to contact you at home, they can do it through your agent's office.

The next category of information on the résumé should pertain to your child's credits and previous experience. When you list your child's credits, start with the best and work your way down. List professional stage, film, and TV credits first, though not necessarily in that order. Indicate the name of the project, the name of the character, where the performance took place, and who directed it. If your child has appeared on local TV and you have a videotape or DVD of that appearance, be sure to write "Tape available."

If your child is just starting out in the business and doesn't have any professional credits, list something good that he's done locally. If he had a lead role in his school show or in a community theater production, that's fine. I don't like to see someone lie on a résumé, because that can come back to haunt you. Every so often I'll receive a résumé from someone from my home area who lists a show that I've not only seen but also worked on. If they've lied about a show that I was involved in, I'll know immediately, since I know who played every role.

I won't tell you that experience doesn't count in this business—it definitely does. The more good credits a child has, the better. Still, I've signed inexperienced children strictly on the basis of ability. It's possible that if your child's credits are modest and he's not outstanding, he may have to go back to a lower level, but that's okay. Everyone starts somewhere. If you're brand new, you may not be quite ready for New York or Hollywood. But in any case, it's always best to be truthful.

It's important that you keep the résumé short and simple. When a casting director turns over your child's picture to look at her résumé he doesn't want to spend an hour trying to weed out the good stuff from the bad. List only the best and most representative things your child has done. Try to show that she's played some good roles. If she's performed leads at the local dinner theater, don't include her ensemble role in the school show. Naturally, you would mention her ensemble role if that is all she's done.

After you've concisely listed your child's credits, list her training—especially if she's had good training. In some cases, a referral by a reputable teacher can help a young performer overcome a lack of experience. Whenever a respected teacher calls and says, "I'm working with a totally inexperienced young girl who I think really has it," I'll see her in a minute. Similarly, if I call a casting director and say, "I've got a new kid who has never done anything, but you've got to see her," his door is always open.

I recently started representing a sixteen-year-old girl named Jane who was sent to me by an acting teacher. Jane never intended to become a professional actress. She had accompanied her friend to a few acting classes, more or less as a favor. Since the classes seemed kind of interesting, Jane signed up herself.

The acting teacher immediately recognized Jane's exceptional potential and referred her to me. Jane arrived at my office with no performing credits or experience whatsoever—not even a show in elementary school or high school. Her only claim to fame was that an acting teacher spotted her talent, told her that she was good enough to work professionally, and referred her to an agent.

Special skills are the last major category to list on your child's résumé. You should include things like tap dancing, jazz dancing, and ice skating. Only list things that your child does well enough to perform. If your daughter rides horseback, list what styles she rides and whether or not she can jump. If your son is a great tennis or hockey player, be sure to include that. Don't neglect more unusual things like windsurfing, juggling, unicycling—anything that might give your child an edge over someone else.

Singers: Choose the Right Songs

Singers need at least two songs to use at an audition. It's better to have more, but certainly no less than a good up-tempo and a good ballad in the right keys—with sheet music arranged in that key. When a singer goes on an audition, she should hand the accompanist music written just the way it is to be performed. She shouldn't say, "I don't sing this part" or "I sing it in another key." Accompanists don't want to hear that. They want the music to be written exactly as it should be played.

It's important for singers to choose songs with which they are comfortable. There should be no notes that might be missed on a bad day and no unfamiliar phrasings. "Don't try to learn a new song the night before," I advise young singers who have musical auditions the next day. "You're not going to be comfortable with the song, and you won't give a good audition. The best song to pick is one that you know inside out, something you can sing really wonderfully."

Singers would also be wise to pick songs that are a little bit obscure. Rarely would I want to hear "Tomorrow" or "New York, New York." I want singers to find something that's recognizable but not something that's going to be done by the three people in front of them and the two behind them. I would never use a piece of original material, though; that's too obscure.

It's very important to choose an appropriate song, not something ridiculous. You wouldn't want to hear a nine-year-old sing something like "My Way" or "What I Did for Love." That kind of thing is ludicrous. When that happens to me, I can barely keep a straight face. A child can give a great audition, but if the people listening are cracking up because the song is inappropriate, a young performer's talent can be overlooked easily.

As I said, I consider two songs the bare minimum. Ideally, though, a singer should have a much larger selection: I'd suggest two or three ballads; two or three up-tempos; something in a rock vein; and something more traditional, such as a Rodgers and Hammerstein or Stephen Sondheim composition. When a singer is that well prepared, I can call and say, "I've lined up an audition for a Broadway show tomorrow. The music is rock. I want you to have two up-tempos and a ballad, and take along some backups in case there's anything else that they want you to do."

Dancers: Learn the Steps That Choreographers Want to See

If your child wants to dance professionally, make sure her dance school is teaching her the names of the fundamental individual steps and how to perform them. That's what choreographers expect. If there's one major problem that I have with dance schools around the country, it's that they spend too much time preparing their students for recitals and competitions and not enough time teaching them how to dance professionally.

"Many young dancers come to auditions without really having learned the dance vocabulary that enables them to hear what's being said and to translate it into the form the choreographer is looking for," one choreographer told me. "Instead, they spend their time looking in the mirror and saying, 'Oh, I look awful there,' or 'I can't do that,' or 'I've never heard of that.'"

Dance students who want to work must be aware that at professional auditions they will not be asked to perform the kind of routine they've done in their recitals. Rather, they'll be asked to do an original **dance combination** of traditional steps. Obviously, they had better know what those steps are. According to one choreographer:

Dance combination:
A series of dance steps created by a choreographer or dancer performed in sequence to counts of music.

"Many professional dancers in New York go to classes five times a week," the late dancer/choreographer Danny Rounds once told me. "When you do that, you can learn a new combination of steps every single week. This kind of intensive work trains you to listen and to pick up the notes (or directions) of the choreographer, such as 'We're going to do a double pirouette to

the right,' or 'Turn in your left foot.' Constantly working with new combinations trains your ability to learn quickly and also trains your ear to listen to what the choreographer is saying, so that you can give him what he wants.

"A great many dance steps have their origins in ballet, but every teacher or choreographer has his own variations. Bob Fosse, for example, did a lot of things turned in, while other choreographers want everything turned out. Before you come into a professional dance audition, you should know the basic steps. When a choreographer calls for a particular step, a dancer should have both the fundamental knowledge of technique and the sensitivity to the choreographer's instructions to be able to do it on demand. Basically, the key to succeeding in the dance business is going in, learning how to pay attention, and not letting yourself get in your own way."

Actors: Be Ready for Anything

Many acting schools place great emphasis on learning **monologues**. In the professional world, however, there are very few times that you're asked to do a monologue as an audition piece. For a young actor, a **cold reading** is really a far more useful skill. At auditions—both in my office and in those of casting directors—children are usually handed a few pages of a script, given a few minutes to look the material over, and then asked to read it. This type of audition is so prevalent today that the ability to recite monologues is no longer that important.

Monologue:

The solo performance of a short scene—usually under five minutes.

Cold reading:

The unrehearsed reading and acting out of a script during an audition.

If a young actor does want to prepare a monologue or two, find pieces that are not too long. Perhaps a good approach would be to memorize two short pieces—one serious and one comic. Make sure the selections are appropriate. The character doesn't necessarily have to be one the child would be able to portray in a show, but the words a child is saying should not sound ridiculous. If an actor is twelve years old, for instance, don't pick something that refers to his four previous lovers. It would be fine, on the other hand, for a twelve- or thirteen-year-old girl to perform a monologue from *The Diary of Anne Frank*, even if she isn't the right physical type for the role. The purpose of a monologue like that would be to demonstrate a young actress's emotional range, so physical characteristics wouldn't be much of a factor. In any case, make sure that the content of the monologue your child selects is appropriate in terms of age and sex. Finding suitable monologues can be difficult, especially for young children. It's really a matter of going through scripts and finding something right.

I want to emphasize again that the ability to handle unrehearsed material on the spot is far more important than memorizing monologues. Peter Golden, head of casting for CBS in Los Angeles, believes that "a wonderful way to get a sense of a young child's talent is to do improvisations with him." He continues:

"We were casting for a new TV series, and we were looking for a little Latin American boy about eight or nine years old. For some reason it was very difficult to find the exact type we wanted. In the course of our talent

search we went to a number of inner-city schools where many of the kids couldn't read that well. In order to find out which ones had natural acting talent, I'd create an imaginary scene and see how each child reacted.

"I'd walk over to a boy and say, 'Look, you've just come into this house, and you've never been in such a big house before. Pretend you're seeing it for the first time and that you've spent your life living out of a car or a small shack. Now just look around this room as if it's a house.' A child who understands what you're talking about will say something like, 'Wow, this is all my place?' And I'll say, 'Yeah, and you can live upstairs, too, because there are two floors.'

"A good, natural young actor can come in, look around, and, without much to say, be able to bring across the truth of never having seen the inside of a house before. When the boy who ended up landing the part did that scene, you believed him every minute."

Because a young actor's natural ability to emote is so important, children are almost always asked to improvise or read something unfamiliar at professional auditions. What it boils down to is this: A child doesn't need to be a great memorizer to be a successful actor. What he needs most is the ability to take any scene an agent or casting director gives him and make it come alive. That's one important reason I always tell my clients: "Be ready for anything."

Moving Ahead—NOTES

- When starting out, don't pay for an expensive photography portfolio. Agents and managers accept snapshots.
- When taking professional pictures, keep your child's hairstyle and clothing simple. The best photos are a straightforward, exact representaton of the child's likeness.
- For safety's sake, it isn't wise to put your home phone number and address on your child's résumé. Many actors subscribe to voice mail services or have pager numbers for that purpose.
- List your child's credits with the best experience at the top. Keep the résumé short and simple.
- Prepare at least two songs (an up-tempo and a ballad) to use at auditions.
- Be prepared to learn an original combination at dance calls.
- Most acting auditions consist of a brief interview and either a cold reading of scenes from the script or improvisation.
- Profiteering is rampant in this business. Early in your child's career your only expenses should be for lessons, pictures, and possibly a demo, and you don't have to spend an extravagant amount on any of these.

5

Finding the Right Representation

I really believe that your relationship with an agent or manager is, in many ways, like a marriage or a close friendship. For your child to have the best representation, you need to find someone with whom you can develop a good rapport and a feeling of mutual trust. Finding the right representative isn't only finding someone who is competent, because there really are quite a few competent agents and managers out there. It's also finding a situation that can evolve into a true partnership.

The person who represents you must be someone you believe in, someone from whom you'll be able to hear both the good and the bad news. Bad news isn't quite so bad when it comes from someone you respect and consider a friend.

It's always exciting for me as an agent when I call a parent to say, "Tyler landed the job." On the other hand, it's really painful when I have to call and say, "Not only didn't Tyler get the job, he also auditioned poorly, and he looked nothing like what they wanted." You're not going to be happy to receive bad news, no matter who delivers it. But if you at least like and trust your agent, you won't feel as if you're being attacked personally.

Mutual trust is probably the most important factor in your day-to-day dealings with an agent. You have to trust your agent to send your child on auditions he's appropriate for and to give you the correct information to prepare him for those auditions. For example, you depend on your agent to tell you what the casting director is looking for and what your child should wear. At the same time, your agent also has to trust and believe in you. She must have faith that you're going to show up prepared and on time. When I send a client on an audition, he is a representative of my agency and a link in maintaining our credibility with the casting office. The prospect of finding representation can be overwhelming if you don't know what you're doing. I'd like to help you avoid confusion by answering some of the questions I'm most often asked about this vital relationship.

How Do I Get My Foot in the Door?

Parents often ask me, "When is the right time to find an agent?" The answer is simple: As soon as you're ready to look for work, you're ready to look for an agent. It's important to help your child work as much as possible during the early stages of his career. To maximize his opportunities, I recommend looking for work on your own while trying to find the best representation you can. Here's how you can get the ball rolling.

Compile a List of Qualified Agents
If you live in a smaller city, you can find the names of competent professionals by calling a local TV station or advertising agency

and asking them who supplies the children that do their shows and commercials. *Ross Report Television & Film* (800-817-3273), a monthly publication, lists New York– and Los Angeles–based franchised talent agents. In other large cities, performing arts unions are your best sources for lists of franchised agents.

The three major unions that franchise agents are SAG (Screen Actors Guild), AFTRA (American Federation of Television and Radio Artists), and AEA (Actors' Equity Association). These unions periodically publish lists of franchised agents in their newsletters. For further information, contact the union representative in your area. If there is no branch of SAG, AFTRA, or AEA in your city, I suggest calling the New York or Los Angeles office and asking for the number of the local office nearest your home.

Actors' unions:

See appendix, page 223.

Set Up Interviews

Once you've compiled your list of agents, your next step is to meet as many as possible. But first you have to make the agents aware of your child by sending a nonreturnable picture, a résumé, and an audiocassette if your child is a singer. Be sure to include a cover letter that lets the agent know about your availability and willingness to travel. I would also suggest mentioning in the letter that you are going to make a follow-up phone call in a week or so. When you make that call, simply say, "I sent my child's picture, résumé, and tape. Can we set up an appointment?"

If you know anyone at all who is connected to an agent, find out if you can use his or her name. Any kind of referral is a very good way of getting your foot in the door. I will almost always see someone who reaches me through a relative, a personal friend, or someone in the business. As helpful as referrals are, though, they aren't absolutely essential. Someone in my agency looks at every submission—solicited or unsolicited—that comes in. If there's any promise at all in the material, it will wind up on an agent's desk.

I personally interview about eight people a week, though I may not take any of them on as clients. Usually one or two of those are based on my receiving promising pictures or tapes in the mail. The others are by referral from professionals or other clients. This approach may not sound particularly innovative, but it is exactly the way successful young performers start out.

Recently I received a phone call from the Mitchum family in Rochester, New York. Their son Timmy was a singer who had performed quite a bit locally. Since they lived quite a long way from New York, I suggested that they send me a package of photos and a videotape of a performance. As soon as I saw the tape I knew that he was special and worth meeting. I called and asked them to come to my office to meet in person. Timmy and his mom and dad rode the bus in from Rochester. He was just as wonderful in person as he was on tape. I immediately called the casting directors for Disney's *The Lion King,* and he went that afternoon to sing for them. After four more trips into Manhattan to sing and act for the *Lion King* director and producers, Timmy has just left with his family to play Young Simba on tour with the **national company** of the show.

National company:

A Broadway production that is scaled down to be taken on tour.

Should I Start Out with a Local Agent?

The decision whether to start out with a local agent or to go right for a big-city agent in New York, Los Angeles, or Chicago depends on how well prepared you and your child are. Most children from smaller cities who make it professionally start out on the local level with a local agent. Still, if your child is ready and you're financially able to go to one of the major cities, you can try to connect with a big-city agency even while she's getting her feet wet locally. If, on the other hand, your child needs more seasoning and your finances are a bit shaky, you might want to try the local level first. The more your child works locally, the more experienced she becomes. At the same time, she can earn money to help finance trips to major cities.

I always encourage my clients to take as much local work as possible. Most good local agents are very supportive and eager to see their children go on to bigger and better things. I work with a number of local agents around the country who regularly send me talent. In a way, it's similar to the minor league farm system used in baseball.

As much as possible, I try not to interfere with a child's local work, but I do have to make the family aware of several things. Be sure that the people who represent your child locally realize that you're auditioning in New York. Since there's a possibility that your child will land a major professional job and have to leave, there should be a backup person prepared to step in for him on short notice. I also advise my clients that once they become union members they are not permitted to accept any nonunion work without permission of the union under whose jurisdiction the job falls.

As I mentioned earlier, there are some talented children who begin working in New York or Los Angeles with virtually no local experience. I've found several such boys and girls at local talent pageants. The parents of these children often are uncertain whether their child is right for the business. By entering their child in a pageant and having him seen by professional evaluators, they receive the feedback and confidence they need to move ahead.

In 2002, I was asked to observe the New York finals of a pageant called Access Broadway. Many of the finalists were exceptional dancers, but one little girl stood out. Courtney Simmons was eight years old and from Atlanta, Georgia. I just had a hunch about her. I invited her to come to my office the next day to read a script for me. She was in the city with her grandmother and they both arrived with big smiles on their faces. Courtney was a bit shy at first, but once she got the script in her hands it was a different story. As I suspected, her reading and—more importantly—her acting were wonderful. Not long after that I sent her to the casting director for the new production of *The Miracle Worker* with Hillary Swank. Courtney beat out a number of New York veterans for the role of Martha. Another career had begun.

Is this unusual? I don't have any exact statistics. But I do know that whenever I judge a talent pageant, I find at least one child who can work professionally. Sometimes I find more than one, but I've never judged a pageant where I haven't found someone who is ready to work in New York.

What Can I Expect Inside the Agent's Office?

If your child has potential and you've followed the guidelines we've been discussing, the chances are good that an agent will ask you to bring him to her office. Here's what you can expect at an initial interview.

Parents often envision walking into an agent's office and having their child receive an uninterrupted audition in a private room. Sorry, that's just not the way it usually is. If you walked into my office in the middle of a typical day, you might wonder how we function in the midst of such tremendous confusion. In my business, the phones are always ringing and people are constantly talking—often in less than subdued tones. Sometimes I'm in the middle of a crisis or a major negotiation. All of that activity is not going to stop just because you and your child have arrived.

In the course of any interview I'm bound to be interrupted at least three times by important phone calls. After I hang up, I expect a child to pick up right where we left off. I understand that interruptions can be disconcerting, and I try to be sympathetic. I'll say, "Remember where we were. Let's try it again. Let's start right here."

Unfortunately, I have no way of knowing what's going to happen when you arrive. If things become too hectic, I might have to stop in the middle of an interview and ask you to come back another day, especially if you don't live too far away. Of course, I try not to do that when people fly in especially to see me. Still, I might say, "I'm just up to my eyebrows right now. Why don't you go out for lunch and come back in an hour?"

I empathize with youngsters who have to concentrate under these conditions, but distractions and interruptions are things that all performers must learn to handle if they're going to audition successfully. Things are bound to be hectic at an audition. While your child is in the middle of her song the casting director may be talking to the person next to him or reading a résumé. That doesn't necessarily mean he doesn't like what your child is doing. Maybe he's already decided that he wants her and doesn't need to listen anymore. In any case, you're not going to know the outcome of an audition until later, so your child had better be able to perform under all kinds of conditions.

In some respects, the noise and frantic pace of an agent's office are a good sign. All that activity means that an agency is busy. If an agent's office is quiet and serene, you might have more reason to worry. When the phone isn't ringing off the hook in my office, we start wondering whether something's wrong. Sometimes we'll even check to see if the phone is out of order or call some other people in the business and say, "Are you dead today, or is there something wrong with our phones?"

Now that you've been warned about the generally chaotic atmosphere of an agent's office, let's take a more specific look at what you can expect.

When a parent and child come to my office for the first time, the receptionist will ask for some basic information about the child—either verbally or on a written form. Then the child will be brought into my office while the parent sits in the waiting room. I don't know of any agency that allows a parent to be present while a child is being interviewed or auditioned. The reason children are interviewed separately from their parents is simple: If a child won't leave his parent to come into my office alone for an initial interview, he's certainly not going to leave his parent to audition for an actual job.

When I first meet a child, I look for the ease with which she handles the situation. Basically, I look for personality first, then I look for talent. I'll start out by asking a youngster to tell me about what she likes to do when she's not performing. I'll encourage her to talk about her family, friends, and pets. I try different things to see if a child is responsive, outgoing, and alert. Sometimes I'll joke around with a youngster I've just met. I'll ask a six-year-old boy if he's married, for example, just to see what kind of reaction he'll have to an off-the-wall question.

If a child is old enough, my next step is to have him read a script for a commercial. When I hand him the script, I'll say, "Look this over for a few minutes. You don't have to memorize it. If you need help with difficult words, you can ask me or your mom." I don't, however, want a child to have any help with interpreting the script. If a child's performance of the script shows promise, I might give him some direction and ask him to do it again, or I may have him tackle some **sides**.

Sides:

Pages or individual scenes taken from a script to be used during an audition or rehearsal. Infrequently, these contain only the lines of a specific acting part with stage directions and cues.

I generally give children as much time as they need to look over their scripts. It's interesting. Some children will look at a script for thirty seconds and say, "I'm ready." Others will take quite a while. I always look to see if a child really is prepared when he begins. Some children don't take as much time with a script as they should. That's an indication to me that the same thing might happen on an audition.

While a child is reading a script—and I expect any child over six to be able to read—I look to see how they take direction, how they develop the character, and how they handle emotion. If a child is under six, I'll pretend with him. I'll make up a situation: "I'm the mommy and you're the little boy." Then I'll say, "Pretend that you've been playing out in the yard and you're very hot and very thirsty. I'm in the kitchen washing the dishes. I want you to come over to me in the kitchen and ask me for a nice cold drink."

Some children have trouble pretending I'm their real mommy. But if a child jumps right into the role, I'll carry the plot out further.

"What would you like to drink?" I'll say. "I have lemonade and apple juice. Which one would you like?" Sometimes I'll try a second imaginary situation and ask a child to act as if she's sick or sad. Commercials for medicine and vitamins often require children to act as if they don't feel well. This kind of role-playing also gives me an indication of how well a smaller child can act.

If at that point I'm interested in representing a child, I'll want to talk to the parent at length. I'll ask a small child to sit in the waiting room, though I may invite a teenager to sit in during my conversation with the parent. If, however, I've gotten an indication during my initial hello to the parent that she's going to be difficult, I might want to see her alone to see just how much trouble I'm going to have. If all seems well, though, I'll bring a fourteen- or fifteen-year-old into the conversation. Then I'll give the parent a verbal evaluation of her child, and we'll discuss the possibility of my representing him.

No matter how impressed I am with a child, I usually suggest that parents see several other agents. When I represent a child, I want an exclusive commitment from the parents. If I'm the first agent they've seen, I'll say, "You may want to see some other agents to know who else is out there. I'm interested in you. If, after you've met some other agents, you want me to represent your child, give me a call." At that point I'll inform the parents of what I expect and give them a **standard union contract** to look over. If they decide to make a commitment to me, they will have to sign the contract sometime in the near future.

Standard union contract:

A legal written agreement between an agent and a performer that is written and approved by the performing arts union involved.

If I'm not interested in a child, I'll honestly try to tell the parent—and often the child as well—why not. If I feel that a child has potential but isn't ready yet, I may ask to see him again in six months to a year. On the other hand, if I feel I'll never be interested, I'll say, "I'm sorry, but I just don't think this will work. Still, I'm not the only agent in New York. Someone else may see something in your child that I'm missing."

Manager or Agent: Which Is Right for Me?

Before you even start looking for representation, you should be aware of the differences between managers and agents—both in terms of how they work and the fees they charge you.

Managers do not submit your child for jobs; they only submit to agents, who then make the submission to casting directors. Generally, you pay an agent 10 percent of your child's salary. If you choose to sign with a manager and work through several agents, you usually pay an additional 15 percent. Some managers charge more, and a very few charge less. But the standard rate is 15 percent. So if you have both a manager and an agent, you're going to be paying at least 25 percent of your child's gross salary in **commissions.**

Commission:
The percentage of a performer's earnings paid to an agent or manager for his or her services.

If you want your child to audition for every commercial for which she may be right, a manager can help by providing access to a variety of reputable agents. Most good "legit" agents—for film, TV, and stage—also have access to a large percentage of commercial jobs. But no one agent knows about all of the TV, film, theater, and commercial calls in New York or Los Angeles.

Another difference between agents and managers is that managers may be more likely to sign an unknown child on the basis of potential. In general, agents usually want children who are ready to go right out on auditions. Since managers stand to make a larger percentage of a child's earnings, they are often more willing to work with a child and help her prepare for auditions. If you've been to several agencies and your child has been rejected because she lacks experience, it might be time to look into a manager.

Managers take at least 15 percent of your child's earnings, so you want to be sure that you're receiving value for those dollars. In many cases that extra expense isn't necessary. Still, if your child wants to work in a lot of commercials or needs help reaching her potential, a manager might be the answer. The best managers do provide a lot of good advice and help and are well worth their fees. But remember: Agents must be licensed by the state as employment agencies and franchised by the unions to submit for union work. Managers, on the other hand, are not licensed, and their activities are not regulated. Therefore, it's up to you to investigate before you sign. I'll talk more about signing with agents and managers in chapter 8.

How Can I Recognize a Ripoff?

Parents who are anxious for their children to work professionally, but know little or nothing about the business, are often ready to jump at any opportunity that comes their way. There exists today a multimillion-dollar vanity industry based on a variety of legal but highly exploitative practices. I'd like to do everything I can to help you avoid these ripoffs.

You should be very wary when anyone tells you that it's going to cost a lot of money to get started. There are some legitimate **nonfranchised local agents** who charge a nominal fee to put your child's picture into their **book of head shots,** and that kind of expense is okay. But I would worry about anyone who insists that you sign an exclusive agreement with a specific photographer for a period of years.

Nonfranchised agents:

Agents not approved by or subject to the rules of the three performing arts unions.

Book of head shots:

A directory of pictures and résumés used by agents or managers to display their clients.

There are a number of so-called management companies out there that promise to get you work. In fact, they are not real managers at all, but fronts that exist only to lure you into spending money on overpriced pictures. These companies stay within the law by sending hundreds of those pictures to reputable agencies and managers, but that's all they do.

In reality, these companies don't care whether or not your child has talent. They buy lists of children's names from hospitals, diaper services, school photographers, and other sources—without any idea of what those children look like. If your child really does have potential, it can be especially self-defeating to sign up with these quasi-legitimate organizations. I receive mailings from these companies all the time, but because I feel that their practices are not ethical, I have no interest in anything they send me. Let me tell you how to spot this kind of scam so you can do what I do with their mailings—throw them right into the garbage can.

First, you'll receive a form letter saying something like this: "Your child has come to my attention as someone who may be right for a career in the big-money world of show business." If you respond to such a letter, a representative of the company will come to your home—usually in the evening when both parents are there. If you buy the sales pitch, you generally have to sign a long-term contract calling for expensive pictures taken by that company's photographer over a period of years. There may also be other fees involved. This whole approach should make you suspicious from the start. For one thing, all the reputable managers and agents I know interview in their offices—never at a family's home.

Be careful if a management company says they are going to do a screen test of your child and it will cost you x amount of dollars. Screen tests cost nothing. If a film company is interested in hiring your child and needs to test him, they pay for the test, not you. They pay to fly you and your child to California if they want to see you; you don't pay for that. Be very careful if someone wants you to pay for something.

Remember this: *Legitimate representatives make no money at all until a child works.* At that point an agent will generally take 10 percent of the child's gross salary. Sometimes nonunion agents in smaller cities may take 15 percent, and this is reasonable. But you should be very suspicious of anyone who asks you to invest thousands, or even hundreds, of dollars before your child has ever landed a job.

In my agency we usually try to find out a family's financial situation and work out some kind of reasonable approach. We can usually find ways to keep the cost of pictures down by using school pictures or working with good photographers who understand the situation. I'm sad to say, though, that there are also other photographers or referral agencies who will tell you, without really meaning it, that your child is beautiful and should be a model. If you take the bait, they'll tell you that you need a port-folio of photos of the child in a variety of poses and outfits cost-ing upward of $600 to $1,000. Believe me, there's no reason on earth why you'd need that kind of portfolio to start out. Remem-ber: you don't need professional pictures until after you've found representation; snapshots work just fine.

I'd like to reemphasize that there are many fine managers and photographers in this business. But, as in many other glamour fields, there is a gigantic vanity industry that exists only to take your money. Unscrupulous people in this field feed upon uninformed parents who are desperate to get their children into show business. At this point I would hope that you are knowledgeable and in-formed enough to avoid such unethical and exploitative practices.

Finding the Right Representation— NOTES

Step 1. Compile a list of agents.

Step 2. Make agents aware of your child.

Step 3. Set up as many in-person interviews as possible.

Step 4. Choose an agent who will do the best job for your child.

Step 5. Avoid people who want to charge you money to get started.

Use the following questions to help evaluate an agent:

• Does the agent specialize in representing children?

- Who are the agent's present and former clients?
- How does the agent feel about your child's potential?
- What kinds of work is the agent going to pursue for your child?
- With which casting directors does the agent have a working relationship?
- How well are you able to communicate with the agent?
- Is your child comfortable with the agent?
- How many clients does the agency represent?
- How long has the agency been in business?

6

Finding Work

Once you find a good agent to represent your child, the real work begins. Parents who are new to the business sometimes think that acceptance by an agent is the same thing as actively landing a job. That's just not the case. Before a child can work, he must go through an extensive audition process each time he is up for a part.

When I submit a client for a particular project, he is first seen by the casting director at what is called a **prescreen**. The casting director will call back the most promising candidates to meet the director. At that point the director may say, "I like these four children. Let's present them to the producer." Then the child will have to face one or more subsequent auditions for a panel that typically includes the producer, the director, and perhaps some executives who are involved with the business end of the project. Ultimately, all these people will put their heads together and make a final decision.

Prescreen:

The first meeting in the audition process between a casting director and a performer.

Understanding the Audition Process

To give you a complete, firsthand view of the entire audition process, I've invited some top casting directors, producers, and directors to join our discussion and share their insights with us. Together we'll try to shed some light on what you and your child can expect.

The casting director is usually the first professional your child will meet outside the agent's office. Although there is a good deal of overlap in the way different show business professionals participate in the audition process, casting directors usually have two key responsibilities: screening out candidates who are not right for a particular part, and keeping a sharp eye out for the special child who can breathe life into that part. Jill Greenberg Sands, Head of Casting for Nickelodeon, explains how people in her line of work function:

"The job of a casting director is to find actors who best suit certain roles in particular projects. It's zeroing in on what a producer and director are looking for and coming up with the most qualified people. For Nickelodeon, we look a lot for a kid who's funny with a strong natural personality and a real kid feel who is also a strong actor. If a kid has a certain spark or energy, but isn't too showbizzy, we really like that. We like to feel that the kid wants to be doing this, that it's his or her passion."

Before a client of mine is seen for a project, I generally have to go through a submission and selection process with the casting director. Here's how that works: Initially, I'll receive either a phone call or a **breakdown sheet** from a particular casting director, describing the characters that are to be cast for an upcoming project. Once the casting director has made his needs known, I'll submit pictures and résumés of clients who may be right for specific roles. After the casting director looks over these submissions and decides who he wants to see, he'll call me to set up audition times.

Breakdown sheet:

A descriptive listing of roles to be cast for a particular production distributed to agents so they can submit appropriate clients for that production.

For this phase of the audition process to go smoothly, there must be a strong feeling of trust between the casting director and the agent. Casting directors I work with regularly trust me to submit only those children who are appropriate for a particular role. Sometimes, if a casting director overlooks a child I feel is right for a certain part, I'll say, "I really think you should see this child." If the casting director respects my judgment, that child will usually get an appointment.

"I must trust that an agent is not wasting my time by sending the wrong children to an audition," says Jill Greenberg Sands. "If a reliable agent tells me that I haven't seen one of her children in eight months and the child has changed a lot, I'll probably take her word and see that child. But some agents will do anything to get the appointment. They treat getting the appointment as an end in itself—that's not what it's all about. The agent–casting director relationship is very similar to the agent–parent relationship: both must

be based on mutual trust and honesty. The same is true for the casting director—producer relationship. Everyone wants honest communication up and down the line."

Once a casting director decides to see a client of mine, I'll call the parent and say something like this: "I have an audition for Ann tomorrow at four P.M. for a television movie that will begin filming in three weeks. The movie is scheduled to appear on ABC next fall. Ann will be auditioning for the role of a twelve-year-old girl who lives in the seventeenth century."

In addition, I might make some suggestions as to what the child should wear and what she should think about ahead of time. Since most auditions are scheduled only a day in advance, you generally won't have much time to prepare. I try to notify families who live far away a few days beforehand whenever I can. But unfortunately, that isn't always possible. Before I send a child on an audition, I usually know a little bit about the **story line** and what kind of character she'll be reading for. If possible, I try to get sides of the script ahead of time so that the child can work on them before the audition. These will either be faxed or e-mailed by our office to the child's home. If I can't get a script in advance, I'll sometimes suggest that the child arrive at the audition a bit early and look over the sides before meeting and reading for the casting director.

Story Line:

The plot outline of a script; a detailed description of what happens to a single character in a script.

"During the audition process the parents need to make sure the child has enough time with the material," says Laura Stanczyk, a respected casting

director whose credits include [*Disney's*] The Lion King, The Sound of Music, *and* A Little Princess. *They should know what the child is expected to do. It's very important that the lines of communication are clear among the casting director, the agent, the manager—if there is one—and the parent. I can't tell you how many times I have kids coming in not knowing they were supposed to have a script, or not knowing that they were to be* off-book.

"When I see that a child has a reading problem, I don't dismiss him because he's not getting the lines right. I'll take the time to do exercises or improvisations. Great kids are not easy to find, so it would be foolish of us to dismiss a child simply because he can't read the scripts. If it's the third time I've called the child back and he still doesn't know the lines, then I realize that this child has a problem that is more than we can deal with."

Off-book:

An actor is off-book when the scene is memorized and the script is no longer needed.

As soon as you arrive at the audition site, check in with the receptionist to confirm that your child's name and audition time are on the list. Anywhere from thirty to a hundred children a day may be seen at a casting session—each with a brief time slot. To avoid confusion, try to show up a few minutes ahead of the scheduled time.

When your child's turn comes, he will be asked to go into the casting director's office by himself. At that point the casting director will conduct a short interview with him to break the ice. She may ask the child how old he is, what he's done in the business, and what his hobbies are. Then the casting director will usually ask the child to read a scene with her. If that goes well, she may give the child some direction to help him interpret the scene in a different way. Meanwhile, you'll be sitting in an outer office with all the other parents whose children are auditioning that day.

---

*"When they first come in the room," says award-winning actor/writer/producer Billy Van Zandt, "I always stand up and shake their hand. We make some small talk about sports or hobbies to see what their personality is like. If we see that they're a little too plastic, we try to work through that. If a kid is phony, he won't get the job. In **sitcoms** we're looking for someone who is the character and who is real. The phony thing may work onstage because you're farther away from the audience, but on camera it doesn't work.*

*"Then we read the scene. I don't care if they have it memorized completely as long as they're familiar with it. I'll always throw in some little direction at the kid even if he is brilliant. If you can't change that reading from how it was done the first time that means the parents have drilled it so far into the child's head it will never be able to be changed. This will usually result in no **callback**. The other thing I want, just like I want for the big guys, is for the child to make a choice, not just read the lines. Even if it's the wrong choice, I need to see a choice. If it's a kid, we usually give him a piece of candy when he's done so he leaves feeling happy."*

Sitcom:
Half-hour situation comedy television series.

Callback:
In the audition process, the request by professionals to see a certain performer again.

Parents often ask, "Can my child land a major part without a track record?" The answer is: Yes, it can happen. Casting directors sometimes conduct extensive regional and even nationwide talent searches when they are trying to find special youngsters. They may run ads in local newspapers or interview children at their schools. As you might expect, the turnout for these open calls is tremendous. Still, if your child makes a favorable impression on the casting director, his career can take off from there.

Douglas Aibel, a respected casting director of such films as *Unfabulous, Signs, The Village,* and *Dead Man Walking,* describes that process:

"In every case the needs of the film and the taste of the director guides the process. I've worked with directors who love the process of finding new, raw talent. I've also worked with directors who are more comfortable with children who have some experience. Wes Anderson was very specific on the feature film The Royal Tenenbaums. *The very first thing he said to me was, 'I don't like working with professional actors, particularly child actors.'*

"In terms of what I look for, I tend to be drawn to children who are very natural and truthful. I tend to work on projects where honesty and quirkiness are valued and slickness and superficiality are not. When I'm working with a child, preparing him to meet the director, I look for someone who is intelligent, inquisitive, truthful, and who really listens to me when I'm acting with him. I look for a child who is malleable.

"Let your child be herself. Don't sit outside the audition room furiously brushing your child's hair. The biggest challenge in auditioning kids is that they come in horribly overprepped, locked into phony ways to say the lines. Have them understand the intention of the scene without giving them moment-to-moment line readings. Let the casting director really guide the process."

One of my clients, Alison Folland, was discovered by a casting director at an open call in Boston during a talent search for the film *To Die For.* She was unknown at the time and not signed with an agent. Ally was later referred to me by the casting director who found her, and she's been working regularly ever since.

How to Help Your Child Audition

Every time your child goes on an audition, it is possible that she will be singled out as the right one for the part. That should give you reason to feel encouraged. On the other hand, you would do well to keep your enthusiasm in check. Learn to stay in the background and confine your role to being a good, supportive parent. The worst thing you can do at an audition is interfere. An agent may sometimes try to advise a pushy or difficult parent, but don't expect the same kind of treatment from casting directors.

"I had a twelve-year-old girl come in recently," says Laura Stanczyk, "and she had on low-slung jeans with her belly button hanging out and tons of makeup on, and I thought, 'Now you're really making me fight. You're making me look past all of this to find the girl.' Other parents go to the opposite extreme. They bring their child in her communion outfit instead of looking like a real child.

"Casting teenagers is even more difficult than casting children. Teens these days have lost that sense of innocence that is needed to portray a teenager on Broadway or in film or TV. That is one of the reasons that we end up casting twenty-two-year-olds to portray teens. They can act the innocence that real teenagers seem to have lost. I don't find many teenagers who are happy about being teenagers these days."

Some parents, in their anxiety to help, overprepare and overre-hearse a child before an audition. This kind of help, no matter how well-intentioned, usually ends up hurting a child's chances. Don't ever tell your child how to read specific lines or what to say in response to a casting director's questions.

"A child should never try to act out his parent's impression of a character," advises **Peter Golden,** *the vice president of Talent and Casting for CBS Television. At an audition a child should only do what he is comfortable doing. After all, he has enough things to deal with and think about without being uncomfortable. Children have a special magic about them. When I see that magic lessened by an interfering parent, it drives me crazy.*

"Sometimes, when I leave the office and I'm waiting for the elevator, I hear parents pumping their children with questions about what went on at the audition: 'What did the casting director say? Why didn't you do it the way we rehearsed?' I've seen any number of children who probably would have gotten the part if it weren't for their parents' interfering. As far as I'm con-cerned, the main thing a parent should tell a child is, 'Be yourself.'"

While there is little you can do to influence the professionals who run auditions, you can make a big difference in how well your child handles these situations. Auditions are stressful, but they need not be traumatic. Never turn the possibility of landing even the greatest part into a do-or-die proposition. Instead, take the heat off your child by planning another activity on the day of an audition, especially if you're traveling a long distance. When my own children were auditioning, I would usually say some-thing like, "First we're going to the audition, then to the American

Museum of Natural History." This kind of planning is important because it makes your child feel that his performance at an
audition is not going to make or break his day—or yours.

---

*"Parents should understand that if their child gave a good audition, they
should be proud of that audition," says Laura Stanczyk. "You should never
assume that your child did anything wrong if he did not get the job. Doing
something wrong is not why kids don't get jobs. It's subjective, it's apples
and oranges, it's, 'I want this shade of green, not that shade of green.' Unless you get specific feedback that your child was scared or frozen up, your
child did nothing wrong. It's more important to ask your child if she had
fun. That will tell you a lot. Be sure to let your child know how great you
think he is, especially when he doesn't get the job. That will keep him feeling
good about himself and let him know that he's not disappointing you when
someone else gets hired.*

*"Once we've settled on two children that we like, the attitude of the parents
comes into play. If, for instance, I've been working with two kids who were
otherwise equal and one set of parents was supportive but the other was a
pain in the neck, I would certainly let the creative people know."*

Before I send new clients on their first major audition, I try my
best to help soften any possible disappointment. I'll say, "Remember, this is your first time, so don't get upset if someone else gets
the part. Just do your very best, and whatever happens, try to feel
good about yourself." No matter what I say, though, there is no
way to make that first audition easy. A child has to go into a room
with one or more complete strangers and perform. That's not an
easy task for a seasoned adult actor, much less a young novice.

"This is probably the hardest profession in the world," admits Peter Golden. "Because when you're turned down, they're not just rejecting something you've written or drawn, they're rejecting you." While he recognizes the inherent difficulties of auditions, Peter offers some constructive suggestions on how to reduce the pressures:

"In this business you have to roll with the punches. There are a lot of different ways that I'll audition children. Sometimes I'll take a lot of time with a child. On other occasions I'll take hardly any time. Whatever happens, you have to walk out the door and go on to the next audition. You may hear from me about the immediate project, or you may see me two or three weeks later for a completely different project. Regardless, you're not being personally rejected.

"Actors often think of auditions as if they were tests, but there's a big difference between, say, a final exam and an audition. In school a teacher generally has little or nothing to lose if a child passes or fails. When a child auditions for a casting director or a producer, however, he's auditioning for people who have everything to lose if he doesn't succeed.

"My greatest hope at any audition is that I'll find someone really good. That's why an actor's attitude walking into an audition should be, 'I'm helping you.' Remember: If a child doesn't audition well, that means I haven't filled the part. And if I don't find children who please the producers, they'll end up accepting something less than what they wanted. Then nobody will be happy. That's why all I want in the world is to have a wonderful child walk into my office and make the part his own."

When a casting director is after a specific type and there are twenty more children waiting to be seen, he is simply not going to spend much time with a child who is obviously wrong for the part. Keep in mind, though, that no matter how right your child is for a particular role or how well he auditions, the chances are that he will be rejected. I constantly have to remind my clients that they wouldn't be represented by my agency if they weren't special. "You can't judge how good you are by whether or not casting people want you," I tell them. "That depends on a lot of things other than how well you can act."

Like most experienced casting directors, Peter Golden has seen young actors lose parts for all sorts of reasons, many of which have no relation to talent or ability:

"A child may get through five callbacks with ten people in the room. Then, at the next audition, there might be twenty people in the room, and one of those people has a problem with the child. That's when it really gets heavy. If that person has veto power over the cast, any number of things can set him off. The child may look just like the bully who beat up the director when he was ten. Believe me, parts are lost for ridiculous reasons like that all the time."

As a parent, it's your job to communicate to your child that casting decisions are basically unpredictable and uncontrollable. I've seen children rejected because the producer or director decided that they were too short, too tall, too blond, too funny-looking, or not funny-looking enough. It's essential that you help your child understand that these things usually have little or nothing to do with how good a performer he is.

Children whose parents remain supportive and take rejection in stride stand a much better chance—both of succeeding in show business and of developing into healthy adults. If your child doesn't land the part, don't ever chastise her by saying, "Why didn't you smile more?" or "I told you to wear the green dress, not the blue one." The child feels disappointed enough in herself without feeling that she's also let you down. If your child walks into the waiting room and tells you that she hasn't landed the part, give her a hug and say something like, "Let's grab a snack and go shopping for that new dress."

By all means, don't be like the parent in this humorous anecdote related by Douglas Aibel: "One of my funniest experiences with a stage mother happened when the door to the audition space opened inwards. I opened the door to send the child back to the mother, and the mother—who had her ear glued to the door—fell into the room. Don't put yourself it that position."

Callbacks

Should a casting director feel that your child is right for a part, he'll be called back to face a series of tougher, more competitive auditions. If it comes down to a choice between five, then two children, there can be even more callbacks. Often a child has to meet several times with different groups of creative and business people who are working on a project before a final decision is reached. The closer a child comes to landing the part, the higher the stakes and the greater the pressure.

The director is often the next person a child will see after he has been approved by the casting director. Directors are generally hired by producers to oversee and shape the creative direction of a particular project. In the case of the original Broadway production *Annie*, however, director Martin Charnin took charge of the entire audition process at the first open call and remained at the helm for the entire run of the show. Here's how he views the director's role:

"A director is first and foremost a quartermaster. Running a successful show is a little like running a war, because there's a lot of traffic that has to be manipulated and handled. The second part of a director's job is that of an editor. In making creative decisions, a director must always be ready to cut out something he may really be in love with for the sake of improving the overall production——be it a song, a moment, a scene, a set, a character, or an actor.

"Finally, a director has to be someone people can trust. Everybody wants to believe that they can count on the director to deal with problems, to be encouraging, to be responsible, and to be there when needed. At different times I find myself functioning as a psychoanalyst, a father, a mother, and a shoulder on which to lean. This doesn't mean that a director always has to be right, but people seem to be happiest when they're able to trust their leader, especially when things get tough."

One Director's Efforts to Humanize the Audition Process

As we just saw, Martin Charnin had an unusual amount of control in the shaping of *Annie*. One of the ways he exercised that control was to structure his auditions as models that he hoped other professionals would follow. "Before I began casting for *Annie*," Charnin recalls, "I thought out the negative aspects of an audition. Then I made specific rules in an attempt to overcome those negatives with positives." He continues:

"Since I began my show business career as an actor in the theater, I knew firsthand what all the negatives were. I remember how awful I felt auditioning—how much pressure I felt to crystallize everything I was into five minutes on that stage. That's a very desperate feeling, because what an actor wants above anything else is the job. I remembered that desperation, and I wanted to eliminate it as much as possible in the Annie auditions. I resolved that no actor—particularly a child—would leave my auditions feeling that way.

"My approach was that children became members of the Annie family the moment they walked into the audition. That was the law for me and for all the people who worked for me. It was the party line. One of the things I did to help reinforce this feeling was to have all the children auditioning on a particular day stand on the stage and sing 'Tomorrow.' I hoped that this kind of approach made all the children feel involved in the Annie experience so that they would leave the audition feeling good about themselves."

Martin Charnin's search for children to cast in *Annie* led to some of the most well-publicized open calls in recent memory. I remember that when he ran an ad in the New York *Daily News* in 1982, looking for a replacement for the lead, several thousand children and their parents lined up in front of Broadway's Alvin Theater (now the Neil Simon Theater). At one point the New York City Police Department was forced to institute riot control procedures. In spite of this potential mob scene, though, Martin was determined to run his auditions with dignity and humanity. To do so, he had to put in some unconventional wrinkles.

"All of the children who were slated to audition on a particular day were asked to come in at the same time," Martin recalls. "The parents were all

invited to sit in the audience at the Alvin Theater and watch their children audition. I had never heard of parents being allowed to view this type of audition, but I hoped that by watching all the kids perform, parents could see for themselves how their children measured up against the competition.

"Once all the parents were seated, I gave a little speech, assuring them that each child would be given an equal opportunity. They were also told that I was not infallible and that it was possible for the most gifted child to escape my notice. By immediately admitting that I could be wrong, I hoped to make the audition experience a much more human one for all concerned."

One of the reasons that Martin Charnin went to such lengths to make *Annie* auditions "textbook models" was his own background as a working actor. But another strong motivation may have been the fact that among the hundreds of children he auditioned— and turned down—was his own daughter. Can you picture how you would feel if you were a director who had to reject your own child? Martin recalls:

Annie *is about the life of an eleven-year-old girl, and this is a very important time in the life of any little girl. I confronted a terrible moment in my own life because my own daughter Sasha was eleven just at the time I was first holding auditions. My daughter, who is now twenty-one, was a very gifted child. Like so many other little girls, she gave a good audition, but she was just too tall for the part of Annie. Imagine how I felt, first having to tell her how good she was and then, in the next moment, why she didn't get the part. This was a demolishing experience for her, and was terrifying for me.*

"Recently Sasha, who is now fashion market director for Allure *magazine, was in Milan for Fashion Week. I got a call from her on her cell phone:*

'Daddy, do you remember when you rejected me for Annie all those years ago and I was so totally upset? Well, you know, I've never really gotten over it. Right now I'm standing in front of Prada, and I know a new Prada bag would definitely make me feel better!' she said with a chuckle.

"Because I was put in the position of having to be both the professional who was delivering the bad news and the consoling parent," Charnin continues, "I became even more acutely aware of how important it was for all children to come away from auditions feeling good about themselves. That's why I tried to make my auditions a positive work experience, learning experience, and emotional experience for each child."

I think it's only fair to point out that not all directors and producers are so sensitive to children and their special needs. Frankly, I cringe when I have to submit my clients for the projects of certain insensitive professionals. There are also some producers and directors who don't work with children very often and therefore aren't that skilled in auditioning them. Still, as more and more roles are written for children, I'm happy to say that a growing number of casting directors, producers, and directors are assuming the kind of attitude that actor/writer/producer Billy Van Zandt expresses:

"I always interview the parents before I interview the kids. These are people you are going to be married to hopefully for five years. If I see that the parents have that desperate 'We've got to pay the rent' look in their eyes and the kid has one eye out the door because he'd rather be playing basketball, then the interview is over. I want to make sure that this is a kid who wants to do this. Let me tell you, for every ten kids that I've seen here in Los Angeles, three of them don't want to be in that room.

"I have some horror stories of parents trying to shove the child through the door. When I hear that going on in the hall I usually tell the parent to take the child home. This is something a child should do because she wants to do it.

"Also, I hate when a child is told to lie about her age. The reality is that if the child is fourteen and looks six, I'll be thrilled to hire her. Don't teach your child to lie."

Final Calls: Getting Down to the Wire

Parents often ask me, "Who has the ultimate say in whether my child gets the part, the producer or the director?" There is no simple answer to this question. In the case of *Annie*, director Martin Charnin was the last word. In many film and TV projects, however, the producer can overrule the director in casting decisions. Billy Van Zandt remembers one situation where the producer was also the star:

"Every set is different. When I worked with Lucille Ball she was tough on the kids. She used to let the parents sit up in the bleachers in the studio during the rehearsal to watch. One time she was working with a little boy. She delivered her line. The kid said something and she said, 'What?' and he answered her. Again she said, 'What?' He said his line over a third time, and she looked up at the parents and said, 'I can't hear him.' This, of course, was a direct line to the parents meaning, 'If he's not louder tomorrow, he's out.'"

The producer's role in most projects is to take money that someone else invests and spend it in the most effective way. "My job is to use that money to manufacture the best possible product," says Caryn Mandabach, who was the producer of *The Cosby Show* and is now an **executive producer** with the Carsey-Werner Company. "To do that, I have to utilize the best equipment and hire the best people." She continues:

Executive producer:
The person in charge of the financial affairs of a production.

---

*"In association with the executive producers and the owners of the show, I hire the director. Normally, I hire the writers. Then I hire the associate producer, the **art director**, the costume designer, and the **stage manager**. Because I'm responsible for spending the money, I hire anybody who has anything to do with the show— that includes the cast. Ultimately I'm responsible for the entire content of the tape that is eventually delivered to the network."*

Art director:
The supervisor responsible for the conception and design of all sets used in a film, commercial, or television production.

Stage manager:
Generally, the head of the production staff who assists the director during rehearsals in technical matters, such as lighting, sets, costumes, etc.

Because producers usually enter into the casting process when the choice is pretty much down to the wire, auditions at that level can be particularly stressful. "The way I see it," says Caryn

Mandabach, "this is the most intimidating and difficult part of the entire audition process. Up till now it's all been preliminary, but this is it—this is make it or break it. Imagine how scary it can be for a child to enter a tiny room and face five grown-ups who are seated at a long table. The five people that a child usually sees at this level are the producer or producers, the director, the casting person, and the head writer. Most of the professionals that I work with are sensitive and concerned about making children feel at ease, but I know that's not always the case. This can be a very frightening situation for a grown-up—let alone a child."

In spite of the tremendous competition for every new role, it is often very hard to find one special child who can breathe life into that role. In fact, when a producer finds a really magical child, she will often try to create a role for him.

If you go back to chapter 1 and review the qualities that will help make a child successful in this business, you'll find that most of the attributes we discussed relate to a youngster's natural talent and his character as a human being. Still, I come across far too many parents who seem to think that their child's show business career hinges on their efforts to make him look and act like their own image of a star. In fact, most producers want children who are real and natural, not those who have been overcoached by their parents.

We've seen how important it is to help children be as well rounded as possible, whether or not they have show business potential. Should you decide to help your child launch a performing career, your efforts to enrich her life and broaden her character are bound to give her an edge—both as a person and as an actor. If, on the other hand, you spend too much time trying to make your child beautiful or perfect, you can hurt her emotionally, and as Billy Van Zandt suggests, you can also hinder her chances at auditions:

"To get the best performance out of a child we try to make it as relaxed as possible. We try to make it a family situation on the set. Among the crew, the cast, and the writers we want it to be a big, functional family that will stay that way for, we always hope, a hundred episodes. The looser we set the atmosphere, the better it is. For a parent this translates into whatever will make your kid more relaxed for an audition, do it. If they work the kid to death on the material beforehand, he's going to come in really tight and on edge from the pressure."

Sensitive producers and directors are skilled at bringing out the magic in a talented but inexperienced child actor. They are also aware, as you should be, that children often need help handling emotions that are threatening or different from what they are feeling at that moment. Caryn Mandabach talks about how parents can help a child overcome this kind of nervousness:

"If a child is having a problem getting into a role, a parent might say, 'They like you; otherwise, you wouldn't have been called back.' Once that is communicated, I would then say, 'Remember, you're not playing you. You're playing someone else who is something like you—except that her mood and attitude are different. So, what you're bringing to the part is not really what you're feeling, but what that character is feeling. After all, you're an actor and that's what an actor does.' Finally, I would tell the child to relax, and if he can't relax, I would encourage him to use that nervousness to good advantage."

Since older children generally have more life experience to draw upon, they aren't as likely to have difficulty making the adjustments that particular roles call for. Very young children are more likely to have problems in this area, according to Caryn:

"When a child is not old enough to read, as was the case with Keshia Knight Pulliam and the other five-year-olds who were competing for the part of Bill Cosby's youngest daughter, the only thing you can do is to ask them to make an adjustment, even if it's only for adjustment's sake. I'll say something like, 'Can you say this as if you're angry at your dad? You're not really angry, you just want to express your point of view.'

"This kind of emotional adjustment can be very difficult for many five-year-olds to grasp. But those children who are talented and aware enough to understand what you're after generally will be able to do anything you ask. In order for a child actor to succeed, her character has to be strong enough to withstand this kind of test. After all, she's going to be tested like that again and again on the job—often under very trying and difficult circumstances."

Guidelines for Successful Auditioning

Now that you've had an overview of the entire audition process, I'd like you to be aware of what you can expect when your child auditions for specific kinds of projects. Since parents often aren't sure which show business field their child is best suited for, I'd like you to understand the requirements for all three major areas: live theater; film and TV work; and commercials. A number of my successful clients do work extensively in all three areas, but most children I meet have qualities that make them more or less well suited to a particular medium.

Live Theater: Your Child in the
Spotlight on an Empty Stage

As Martin Charnin pointed out, auditions for major theatrical productions can be frightening—particularly for children who have never had that experience. Imagine how intimidated you would feel if you were asked to stand alone on a Broadway stage, look out into the vastness of an empty theater, and then deliver your lines with poise and assurance. That's the kind of pressure children often have to face at theatrical auditions. Once in a great while a sensitive director will go out of his way to make the audition setting less frightening, but you had better not count on that. The best way to help your child handle this difficult situation is to talk to him and let him know exactly what to expect.

At auditions for Broadway shows, all the children who are going to be seen that day are gathered backstage with the stage manager. As each child's turn comes up, the stage manager sends him out on the stage all alone and directs him to stand center stage facing the audience. The stage lights are then focused on the child, while the faceless voice of the director says from somewhere in the audience, "Please give us your name and tell us how old you are." Then the child is asked to read his lines and the stage manager reads the other parts. When the child finishes, he may be given some direction and asked to read the same lines again. If the director has heard enough on the first reading, he will just say, "Thank you," which is often just a polite way of saying, "No, thank you."

When I was new to the business, I had to watch my twelve-year-old son Stephen go through this same ordeal. Believe me, it was very tough on both of us. I'm sure that the entire situation would have been a lot less traumatic if someone had described the procedure to us in advance.

We've talked about how important it is for a child to be natural at auditions—to be himself. In TV and film work that "real" quality often overshadows everything else. In live theater, however, a child's technique and professional experience can put him at an advantage. "When you work on camera," I tell new clients, "you have to make everything smaller than it actually is because you're so much closer to that camera lens than you would be to anyone looking at you in real life. But when you're on stage, it's just the opposite. In live situations you have to make everything bigger than it really is for people in the audience to see what you're doing."

To work in live theater, a child must be able to master his lines and say them exactly as they are written. He must also be able to move around the stage with confidence and respond appropriately to what the other actors are saying and doing. Ultimately, a young actor must have the ability to direct his performance toward an audience without being obvious about it. These are skills that require some amount of training and technique.

We've seen that it's not unusual for inexperienced children to be discovered at open calls and cast for major films and TV projects. But, as casting director Peter Golden notes, this is less often the case when it comes to casting for a major theatrical production:

"We often used inexperienced children on The Cosby Show *because technique really doesn't matter all that much when you're filming or videotaping. But when I was casting for the Broadway shows* Nine *and* Peter Pan, *we hired only children with lots of experience and years of music and dance training. Mistakes due to a lack of technique are relatively easy to correct when you're working on a film or TV project. But there aren't many producers who are willing to take an inexperienced child out of junior high and trust him with the lead in a fourteen-million-dollar Broadway production."*

Child actors who have the technique and pizzazz to work on-stage sometimes have difficulty retaining enough of the understated, natural quality that is needed to work well on camera. In guiding your child through the early stages of his career, be aware that there is a fine line between gaining technique and losing a natural, child-like quality. You can help your child develop into a versatile professional by seeking out training and performing experiences that enhance his character, even as they sharpen his professional skills.

Film and TV: Helping Your Child Keep It Together in Front of the Camera

For film and TV auditions, children are generally videotaped or screen-tested no later than the first callback. Today, being screen-tested doesn't mean flying out to Hollywood, working on a soundstage, and filming a lengthy scene. Ninety-eight percent of the time, children are asked to put the same short scene on video-tape that they performed live for the casting director at the pre-screen. Then the producer, director, and others involved in the final decision compare the videotapes of all the children who are auditioning for the same part before making their choice.

One of the most important things to remember in working in front of the camera in film and TV projects is: *Don't look at the camera.* An actor should never think about how she's being photographed, because that's really none of her business, at least not until later.

When my clients are auditioning for a film or TV project, here's how I prepare them: "Unless you're told otherwise, don't look at the camera, don't look at the **TV monitor,** and don't look at the people who are auditioning you. Be sure to keep your head up off the page when delivering your lines, and don't worry about giving a perfect reading. Try to think of the scene you are playing as something that is really happening in your life, and just go for it."

TV monitor:

A television set that only shows what is being seen by the director during filming or videotaping.

For commercials, actors are usually required to face the camera. But in most dramatic situations an actor isn't talking to the viewer; he's talking to the other actors who are involved in that scene. At an audition a child has to be able to imagine that those other actors are actually there with him and project that reality to the decisionmaking panel. Since children who are trained for the theater are taught to do everything "big," they often have to be retrained to bring things down when they work on camera.

"The most common mistakes children make on camera are that they try too hard, overact, and move around too much," says one casting director. "When actors read scenes live, they often tend to exaggerate their movements and gestures. That approach may be okay for theatrical work, but when the camera is on, it's important not to play things too big.

*"When I audition people, I will **zoom in** the camera from a **long shot** right into a **close-up**. Since most on-camera acting takes place in a close-up, I want to get a sense of how a child thinks. When you're thinking, you don't have to move a muscle. That's why the way a child projects stillness is very important. I don't want children to be wooden, but I also don't want them to bob their heads or move around a great deal."*

Zoom in:

A term used to instruct a cameraman to move in closer on a person or object without moving the camera. This is accomplished by using a special "zoom" lens.

Long shot:

A camera shot in which the subject is seen at a distance; a shot that includes all of a subject and part of the detail of the scene.

Close-up:

A camera term used by a director when he or she wants only the face and shoulders of a performer to appear on the screen.

I've seen some children who have a very good natural quality in person but who seem to have difficulty getting that quality across on film. When your child auditions for film or TV—especially for a lead role—the professionals who see him will all be asking themselves the same basic question: Does that child have the presence and charisma to hold an audience's attention every minute he is on-screen? Jane Milmore of Van Zandt/Milmore Productions talks about videotaped auditions from her perspective:

"Tapes in general are hard. When I'm casting children, I usually want to see them in person unless they're from across the country. When we were casting the pilot Staten Island, 10309, *we must have watched twenty-five hours of tape to cast the lead fourteen-year-old boy. If we don't see what we want in the first few seconds of an audition, we fast-forward to the next person. In the case of* Staten Island, *we were sitting on the floor, going through pictures, with the tape running in the background. Every so often we would look up at the screen. Then we heard David Krumholtz. We stopped what we were doing and reran the tape. We actually ran it over and over. He was perfect for the role. I said, 'We have to get him out here.' We flew him to Los Angeles and he ended up with the part."*

Commercials: Selling the Product
Is the Most Important Thing

I'd like to turn our attention to TV commercials—an area of show business that I know is of great interest to many young performers and their parents. Though there are many similarities between commercial and other kinds of auditions, there are also several important differences. Bonnie Deroski talks about the qualities a child needs to work in commercials:

"In most TV shows, movies, and plays, there is usually time for an audience to get to know a character. With commercials, however, there is virtually no time for character development. Commercials today are designed to catch viewers' attention before they can grab the remote and change the channel, and an actor's face may appear on-screen for only a few seconds.

"To work in commercials, children need to have an open, attractive look and—most importantly—an 'instant' personality. In fact, commercial directors often fast-forward through the audition tape to see who catches their eye. At that point, they will slow down the tape and watch through the actor's full audition. You can see that if a child's opportunity to make an impression is momentary, then it stands to reason that if the child doesn't 'pop' on the small screen, his chances for a callback, let alone a booking, are next to nil.

"If a child walks up to you and immediately starts talking your ear off, if he's vibrant and animated—if you can't take your eyes off him—that's the kind of child that is needed for television work. In terms of look, the requirements are even less specific than that. Advertisers don't always hire

children who are exceptionally beautiful. Children with a friendly, all-American look always seem to be in demand, but depending on the project, I receive calls for any given physical or ethnic type.

"However, there is one tiny physical flaw that can make the difference in a child's marketability for commercials: crooked or missing teeth. With the extreme close-ups used for television and especially in advertising food products, nice teeth are critical for many castings. And this is a special consideration as children grow and naturally lose their baby teeth. Temporary teeth, known as 'flippers' (they flip in alongside the real teeth), can be made on demand by a dentist for a nominal fee."

In commercials, perhaps more than any other area of show business, a child's natural personality is the key to success. In a film, play, or TV show, a child might be asked to assume another personality. But in commercials, producers basically want children to play themselves. Advertisers aren't interested in children who can act in the usual sense of the word. What they are looking for is a unique child, one whose real personality will come across to the viewer and ultimately sell the product. According to Bonnie:

"While it's true that children who land major parts in films and TV series must have genuine talent and acting ability, children who succeed in commercials may or may not be talented actors. I can think of quite a few children who experienced great success doing commercials but never booked a movie or TV series.

"Many extremely talented young actors who are regularly hired elsewhere in the industry for being able to interpret a script, portray a character,

or sell a song don't really have the right temperament for commercial act-
ing. It takes a camera-ready face and spontaneous attitude to book TV
commercials.

"On the other hand, acting ability can definitely help in many instances. I
often get calls from casting directors who tell me they are looking for 'real
kids,' or what I interpret to mean actors who don't seem to be acting. And
unlike other types of auditions, children auditioning for commercials rarely
get the script in advance. Children who are accustomed to memorizing lines
quickly and have lots of acting experience have an advantage in these in-
stances. And then there are those exceptional commercials where the child
talks right to the audience for the entire spot. For this type of job, children
who have the right look, great personality, and *acting ability overwhelm-*
ingly have the better chance of being considered."

Since most commercial auditions are videotaped, a child
should have some idea of how to relate to the camera before he
walks in. Many parents correctly sense that their children have the
right kind of look and personality to work in commercials. But
for a child to be successful, those natural qualities must come
across on the TV screen. To become a professional commercial actor, a child must possess a natural gift that is developed through
experience. Bonnie says:

"Lots of kids can be very unaffected meeting with me in my office, but when
they go on their first audition in front of a video camera, they come across
stiff and uncomfortable. Sometimes children can start out by 'acting' their
way through on-camera auditions and after a few tries can learn how to be-
have naturally. But, unfortunately, for some children, the pressure of being

*recorded overshadows their ability to be themselves. It is this child who will
become discouraged by the commercial audition experience."*

While it's true that many children break into commercials
without much training or experience, the ones who work regularly
have the attributes we've been talking about in this section and
elsewhere. The opportunities for children in commercials—as well
as in theater, films, and TV shows—are greater now than ever before, but so is the competition. I've seen too many well-meaning
but overeager parents build up their hopes and spend their money
without first realistically evaluating their child's potential and developing a workable, step-by-step plan. I strongly suggest that you
follow the guidelines we've discussed in these first six chapters before you buy that plane ticket to Hollywood or New York.

Finding Work—NOTES

- The job of a casting director is to find actors who best
  suit certain roles in particular projects. Often the
  producer makes the final casting decisions.
- Don't overprepare and overrehearse your child before an
  audition.
- Remain supportive of your child and take rejection in
  stride. Casting decisions are basically unpredictable and
  uncontrollable.
- Talk to your child before each audition and let him know
  what to expect.
- Children auditioning on camera should be careful not to
  try too hard, overact, or move around too much.

- In commercials, a child's natural personality is the key to success.
- The opportunities for children in commercials, as well as in theater, films, and TV shows, are greater now than ever before—but so is the competition.

7

Making It in the Music Scene

Hillary Duff, Britney Spears, Brandi, Justin Timberlake, Destiny's Child, Lindsay Lohan, Billy Gilman, Christina Aguilera, and Usher—the list goes on and on. These are kids who have had gold albums on their wall before they had a high school diploma. When I started as an agent in 1978 it was rare for a kid to achieve stardom in the music business. Little girls and boys dreamed of having their own TV series or of becoming the next Annie on Broadway. All of this has changed in recent years with the explosion of young faces in the recording industry. Every little girl who sings now fantasizes about becoming a huge pop star.

VHI has a series that they created called *Driven*. Produced in part by Beth Melillo, *Driven*, as described by VHI, "brings the music world's biggest pop icons' unknown pasts to life with footage that the public has never seen" as well as "interviews with those special people who played integral parts in their development." As I mentioned in earlier chapters, I helped Britney Spears begin her career. Therefore, I'm one of those "special people" in the Britney episode. I can always tell when that episode has been rerun because I am deluged with mail, phone calls, cassettes, CDs, and videotapes from girls and their parents. The message is always the same: "Wait until you hear my daughter. Please, please see her. You won't believe how talented she is. She's the next Britney Spears."

First of all, there is no "next Britney Spears." There already is a Britney Spears. There's also a Christina, a Justin, a Brandi, a Lindsay, and so forth. The next child pop star will be someone new, with a new face and a new sound. It is possible that new face and sound could be your daughter's or son's.

There are far more opportunities for pop performers today than there were even a decade ago. With the explosion of the Internet and the galloping growth of cable TV channels, there are certainly more outlets for pop performers. Still, the competition is stiff—your child has a much better chance of landing a role on TV or in a film than of "hitting"—the music industry term for making it big. Brian Lukow, who produced the group Dream Street and is now producing the new girl group Huckapoo, says that when he was casting the latter, he was amazed at the number of submissions he got—many of those from professional talent representatives. "I would contact the parents to set up an audition and they would tell me how impressed I would be with their child," Brian says. "I wondered if they realized just how huge the talent pool is out there and actually knew their kid's level of talent."

It's a tough area of the business to crack, and once you do hit both you and your child will need a lot of emotional and physical stamina to maintain that level of stardom. In order for me to help you understand why, I need to explain how the music industry differs from other areas of show business.

A Pop Star Must Be Multitalented

It's a given that today's pop hopefuls must be well above average in the cute or pretty departments. But that's not enough. It's not even enough to be able to sing, or to dance, or to act, or to play a musical instrument. Today's young pop stars often must have— or acquire—*all* of those skills because the pop world has spread into multiple media. Look at the various activities over the past few years of people like Hillary Duff and Nick Cannon. Today's up-and-comers may be expected to do a sitcom, a music video, a record, a film, *and* a tour of live performances.

It's a Nocturnal Business

Because most live performances are at night, the musicians, producers, and crew a pop artist works with tend to be night owls, working till the wee hours and sleeping till early afternoon. That is obviously not the ideal lifestyle for a minor—especially one who is still growing and going to school.

The Music Business Is Not as Regulated as Other Segments of the Entertainment Industry

At this point, there is little union protection for budding or working pop artists, which can leave them vulnerable to con artists and—especially critical for minors—without legal mandates and protections. "While some major record labels do have arrangements with AFTRA and the American Federation of Musicians, those unions allow the labels to waive certain conditions," says manager/producer Bert Price, who is currently working with the group Imajin. There is also, of course, the little matter of having to be signed by such a label before you are afforded any union protection at all.

"The recording industry is in many ways like the Wild West," agrees Alan Simon of On Location Education. "Let's take, for example, a pop group that is touring the United States. The rules governing when and how much the members of the group can work and what must be provided for them, such as education, can literally change as soon as the group crosses a state border, and some states provide only a smattering of applicable state law."

In terms of minors getting an education, Alan says, the multifaceted nature of today's pop business also becomes an issue. He continues:

"Let's say the group does a show that ends at eleven P.M. Then they get on the bus. Everybody falls asleep until they roll into the next town on the tour around four or five in the morning. They check into the hotel, get a couple more hours of sleep, then they do the local Z-Morning Zoo radio show. After that, the teacher is not the only one waiting to work with the kids. There are also vocal trainers, choreographers, nutritionists—a whole entourage of people jockeying for the limited amount of time that's available."

Fortunately, Alan says, the situation is beginning to change for minors in the pop business. While California has long had the country's strictest rules governing the lives and interests of child performers, New York—the other big entertainment industry state—has recently jumped on the bandwagon. On March 28,

2004, New York's Child Performer Education and Trust Act of 2003 went into effect. As explained in an earlier chapter, the law requires the deposit of 15 percent of a child's income into a trust account and sets mandatory educational standards. "Education for child performers always should have been a New York State mandate but in reality it never was before now," says Alan, who adds:

"With the advent of this law there's likely a movement under way—if not on a state-to-state basis, but certainly on the federal level—to try to undo the effects of the Federal Labor Act of 1938, which, for whatever reason, did not cover children in the entertainment industry. Newsboys are covered by that law; performers are not.

"The long and short of it is, I can only hope we're on the right footing to be able to do right by the kids. Time and time again I've come across kids who have landed recording contracts and who aren't necessarily the most stellar of students, kids who tend to believe that they don't need an education, that they don't need anyone to tell them how to save or spend their money. And then when they don't hit—and they aren't given a whole lot of time to hit—they end up absolutely nowhere."

Limited Regulations

In this business, you work with managers and producers. We will talk about their roles in more depth later in this chapter but for now, suffice it to say that a manager handles a client's business affairs and obtains work for her, and a producer helps her create and record her music. Traditional talent agents play almost no part in the music business, though we are occasionally called by producers looking to "cast" musical groups for which they already have a concept and a business plan. That's how my client Lindsay Nyman became a part of the new girl group Huckapoo.

I know many first-rate, successful managers and producers who pride themselves on their honesty and integrity. The problem is, just about anyone can hang out a shingle without having to adhere to standards set by a professional organization or by one of the unions—as I'm required to do, for example, as a Screen Actors Guild–franchised talent agent. For this reason, there is a lot of profiteering in the business. Many a hopeful has shelled out an absurdly inflated amount, for, say, pictures or a **demo** and ended up pretty much right back where she started from.

Demo:

A recording of your child performing to give to a professional who doesn't need to hear a finished product.

Money Is Tighter

At least it is in the early years of a pop career. When your child lands a theatrical, film, or TV part, you can expect that she'll be paid reasonably soon after she begins working. That's not how it works in the music business, however. "What is spent on one day of the production of a film or three or four days in television equates to the recording fund of an *entire album*," says manager/producer Bert Price. "The average recording deal from a label these days is two hundred and fifty thousand dollars."

That may sound like a lot, but keep in mind, Bert says, that this **advance** must be split among *everyone* involved in the project—the artist, manager, producer, attorney, and so forth. How much goes where is spelled out in the contract. The artist may be allocated $50,000 for living expenses—perhaps $25,000 up front and $25,000 when the album is completed. And no one gets any more money until the label has recouped its initial investment from income the individual or group brings in.

Advance:

In the recording industry, the amount paid up front by a recording company to an artist and her team to cover costs while a record is being made. The company recoups this payment from record sales.

The other thing to keep in mind is that making an album may take a long time—much longer than you might have imagined—which leads us to one last but important point in this section:

The Time Commitment

I believe the best way to illustrate this is by recounting the creation and launch of Huckapoo, the new five-girl group produced by Brian Lukow.

Birth of a Girl Group

By the time Brian Lukow started casting Huckapoo in September 2003, he already had the concept of the group all mapped out. He wanted five girls between the ages of thirteen and fifteen and each would represent a different musical persona—a punk rocker, a hip-hopper, and so on. "Because of some prior bad experiences, I made sure that the kids and the parents understood the commitment right up front while I was casting," he says. In February 2004, the girls who had been cast went to work in earnest. Brian continues:

"The girls worked five days a week. A typical day for them began with a long commute with a parent, because the girls live on Long Island and in Connecticut and Pennsylvania. When they arrived at the studio, they were tutored in their studies every day from ten-thirty to one-thirty. Next came a lunch break. After that they worked almost constantly—learning choreography, rehearsing, recording, doing press interviews or a photo shoot, preparing for a video . . . and most days they did all of the above. We finished up at seven-thirty or eight P.M., at which point the girls and their parents began the commute home. We did record on some weekends, but we kept everything within the legal limits set for minors. You don't want to overwork kids because it's counterproductive. You want to maintain their interest and excitement."

The result of all of this determination and hard work? By mid-May 2004 (when this book went to press) the group had recorded twenty-four songs. At the time, Brian said, "That means we recorded at a rate of about two songs every single week, which is an outstanding amount. My goal was to get as much accomplished as possible in May because I knew that the girls would be taking their school finals in June and would be less available to me."

Brian's other goal was to get the album finished and in the

stores by the back-to-school season in September 2004, and that would be after Huckapoo completed a summer tour of state fairs, malls, summer camps, and other small venues "to find out what's working and what's not," as Brian put it. When I spoke to him in May, he said he felt pretty confident the group could achieve that September goal. "And if it happens," he added, "I will jump up and down because that would be an incredible accomplishment. It would mean we went from issuing the first casting notice to putting the album in stores in the space of one year."

As a comparison, Brain recounts his experience with producing Dream Street. "The initial casting of Dream Street was in June 1998," he says. "We had to recast the group in January 1999. There were a lot of roadblocks and the first record didn't come out till July 2001. It took thirty-seven months—more than three years."

I asked Brian which scenario was more common— Huckapoo's or Dream Street's? "Typically," he says, "it's somewhere in the middle—about two years of development prior to an album's release." And that feels like forever if you're only in your teens.

The Winning Qualities

I hope I haven't scared everybody off. Yes, it's a tough business, but if your child is really determined to make her mark in it . . . well, try to think of it the way you think about buying a lottery ticket: *Someone* has to win.

Speaking of winners, I asked several industry insiders just what qualities today's pop superstars appear to have in common. Brian Lukow neatly sums up the consensus: "The really great ones have a combination of three things—the talent, the desire, and the right parent," he says. "To me, that's the triple threat."

I asked my sources to define the "right parent." "Among the stars, I have consistently seen that the parent is supportive and determined but not to the point of being an overbearing stage mother," says Beth Melillo, who produced VH1's *Driven* and now works on other TV and film projects. Casting director Matt Casella, who eventually cast Britney Spears, Justin Timberlake, and Christina Aguilera, among many other familiar names, in Disney's 1990s version of *The Mickey Mouse Club,* provides one good example of the right balance. As you may recall, he didn't cast Britney initially because he felt she was too young. "Every week, however, her mom, Lynn, gave me a call. She'd say, 'We understand Britney didn't get on the show and you're not testing her, but she's just itchin' to get out of Kentwood and to get professional experience. Can you help us?'" At that point, Matt referred her to me.

Beth Melillo continues: "The reason these parents worked so hard for their children is that they saw a talent and didn't trust anyone else handling their children's work. They groomed those children, whether it was driving them every night to dance class or combing the ads for auditions and jobs. And for some reason they were always very in tune emotionally with their children. They understood and supported their children's drive. Pink's family, for example, understood why she stayed out late many nights singing at clubs ... they understood that she *had* to do it—that she was driven."

Matt Casella also mentions what he terms that "strong connection" successful performers seem to have with their parents. "This was because from very early in their children's lives the parents were guiding their careers and were with them so much, protecting them like a mother lioness protects her cubs," Matt says. "Even now, when many pop superstars have reached their early twenties, you will see that their parents are still very instrumental in their careers, their lives, and in their sanity. Britney's mother went everywhere with her; Justin's mother was everywhere with him."

Talent, desire, and your staunch support—if your child has these things going for her, she's ready to start her pop career. In the next section, we'll discuss how to begin.

Getting Discovered

Even my own ten-year-old granddaughter has asked me, "How do you get discovered as a pop star?"

First of all, I really, really dislike the term "getting discovered"— mainly because most people have a completely unrealistic and fairy-tale notion of what this means. Those old movies in which some small-town girl is spotted by a traveling talent scout, is whisked to Hollywood, and becomes America's Sweetheart within weeks (and usually ends up treating everyone in her life like dirt!) are just that: movies. Fiction. In reality, it takes years to become an "overnight sensation."

Remember, Britney Spears came to me when she was only eight years old, and even then she was already a veteran of performances at county fairs and other local venues. Subsequently, she spent years taking lessons to perfect her various crafts and playing parts in commercials and television to gain experience and exposure before she emerged as the pop sensation we know today.

I like Matt Casella's definition of "being discovered." Matt held open auditions (that is, *anyone* could try out) all over the country to cast *The Mickey Mouse Club*, and several of those kids went on to fame and fortune. "In many cases, I was the first professional casting director these kids had ever met," Matt says. "The way I think about it is not that I 'discovered' them but that I created a bridge from their small town to the big time."

So how do you make it to that "bridge"? What does your child need to do in order to ace such an audition?

Assess Your Child's Musical Tastes and Talent Level

You want your child to sing country-western, but the only genre she likes to sing is pop. Give in, according to producer Beth Melillo. Most talented kids know where their talent lies, she says, and if they're forced to expend their efforts elsewhere, they just won't last. Beth says that Jay-Z's mother used to dismiss all of his banging with spoons on the kitchen table as "noise." What she didn't understand at first was that this was the type of music Jay-Z loved and at which he excelled—rap!

Once you and your child have narrowed in on a specific music style, it's time to get an honest appraisal of your child's talent and potential. Don't go to Grandma for this, because Grandma would applaud even if your Emily screeched "The Star-Spangled Banner" at the top of her lungs (à la Roseanne!). Seek someone with a musical background, such as your church's choir director or the music or band teacher at your child's school. You might even consult a voice teacher or a local talent agent—but be careful. If you spend enough money, *somebody* will tell you exactly what you want to hear. This is why you should get several opinions . . . and most of those should be *objective* opinions; that is, from people who have nothing to gain financially from your child.

Arrange for the Right Lessons

Don't be dismayed if someone whose opinion you value suggests lessons. Every aspiring pop star needs first and foremost to learn how to sing on key and stay on that key, and proper breath control. These abilities aren't necessarily inherent in a talented child.

When little kids come into my office and don't have their own music I ask them to sing "Happy Birthday." It's a great test . . . because in actuality it's a hard song to sing. If a child sings it once and misses that octave jump (at " . . . happy BIRTHday, dear Sarah"), I sing it for her correctly. If she sings it correctly the second time, I know she's got potential and can learn to sing.

Try to find a voice teacher who specializes in the kind of music your child wants to sing. Ask potential teachers who some of their other clients are. If those clients are primarily theater types, you might want to look elsewhere, because a Broadway voice isn't compatible with pop music. When Britney Spears came to me she had a big, belty Broadway voice—that's the style she'd been taught—and her repertoire consisted of old classics like "Bye-Bye Blackbird," "Coronet Man," and Johnny Ray's "Cry." She found her pop voice while doing *The Mickey Mouse Club*, and over the years producers and vocal coaches helped her develop the kind of breathy sound she has now.

Brian Lukow, the Huckapoo producer, has often encountered the same problem:

"In the last year, I've probably auditioned 250 girls and, over the last several years, just as many boys, and I've found that a lot of them have been trained to sing from a theater point of view. I call it 'The Ethel Merman Factor.' These kids have trouble with the up-tempo type of songs that usually constitute pop. They sing them incorrectly.

"But they can be retrained. One of the Huckapoo girls switched from a theatrical music coach to a coach who had worked with Jon Bon Jovi and other big pop stars and she's doing fine."

In this age in which pop stars must be multitalented, dance lessons are also a solid investment. In this case, too, many children take the wrong kind of classes. Says Brian:

"The best kind of classes are those that involve a lot of movement—whether it's just a movement class or a hip-hop class. While there's a shortage of this kind of training, many dance studios offer it. Pop producers don't look for lyrical dancers per se—we look for kids with movement skills. A lot of that is God-given like anything else, but much of it can be taught."

Ironically, since New York City is one of the most expensive cities in the world, you'll probably find the least expensive dance classes here, because so many performers live here and there's a lot of competition for their business. I know of one New York dance school that charges as little as fifteen dollars per class. This is one of the reasons I often recommend that a young performer from elsewhere spend a summer in New York City.

You might also encourage your child to learn how to play a musical instrument. Says manager/producer Bert Price, "I personally feel that every singer should know something about the piano. It's important to know the basic fundamentals of music."

Establish a Look and a Sound

Your child needs to keep up on the marketplace. She needs to know what's now and even what's not quite now but will be. She needs to be familiar with the current sound and to find her place in that sound. She has to know what's hip and to dress hip, but she also should strive for a bit of individuality that will make her stand out. Lots of people, for example, clearly remember the cute, black and white hat Britney Spears wore when she auditioned for *The Mickey Mouse Club* the second time around.

Get Experience and Exposure

Encourage your child to sing and dance in public at every opportunity. Have her sing in her school chorus; get involved in a community production or a dinner theater; sign up to perform at the local county fair; compete in her school's annual talent show; sing in clubs if there are no age restrictions. As pop manager/producer Bert Price reminds us, "There are talent scouts all over the country."

I can back that up: I've found clients, for example, singing in church choirs, because the choir is such a good source of musical learning. Choir directors are often very well-trained people who have gone to good music schools but decided not to go on to professional careers. They usually make excellent voice teachers.

Even performances that don't involve singing and dancing are good experience for your child because they help develop and hone her acting skills and allow her to become accustomed to performing in front of an audience. Ben Affleck was a sixteen-year-old client of mine who was performing in his high school play, *Alice in Wonderland*, when I introduced him to Matt Casella. If your child doesn't land an acting role, encourage her to join the crew—paint scenery, work on the lights, hand out programs. If she's older, she might seek out an internship at a local talent agency. She may meet professional contacts, and these activities will also give her a taste of what the entertainment industry is all about.

What about the pageant circuit? Matt has mixed feelings. "I'm not a big fan of pageants," he says flatly. "I recently watched a reality TV show that featured one poor child whose mother had spent two thousand dollars to enter her in a local pageant. The child won third or fourth place, eighty dollars, and a trophy—what a scam! This is exploitation. On the other hand, kids *do* have to perform in them, and they learn regimen, routine, and rejection."

Audition!

When Brian Lukow was casting Huckapoo, he was stunned by the number of submissions sent to him in advance that included a video or other visual medium showing the potential auditioner performing. "My new rule is not to watch these at all because in ninety-five percent of the cases, it negatively predisposes me to the people before they come in," Brian says. "The best thing to do to show off your talent is to audition live."

While many auditions in the entertainment industry require that a performer be referred by an agent, this is much less the case in the music business. Look for notices of open auditions and try to sign up your child for every *legitimate* (and we'll talk about this word shortly) one she fits the requirements for. When Matt Casella held open auditions for *The Mickey Mouse Club* in cities throughout the United States, he would try to get the word out in advance with a blitz of publicity before he arrived in each city. He would do local TV, newspaper, and radio interviews, and place ads as well. Keep your eyes and ears open for these opportunities. I have also seen open auditions publicized in local parenting magazines such as *L.A. Parent*. Entertainment industry trade publications (see the Appendix) can sometimes be a source as well.

Matt offers a word of caution here: "I don't want to encourage people to go to *every* audition they hear or read about, because half of them are a racket. The audition is really just to get you to sign up for classes or something like that. The only things you should have to spend money for early in your child's career are for lessons, for pictures—to leave at auditions and so forth—and for a demo." (We'll be discussing demos in a page or two.)

To avoid getting scammed, Matt strongly advises that you rely on good word of mouth and/or that you research the company or the individual before you sign up for an audition. Checking with the Better Business Bureau in the area is a good idea. The Internet is another excellent place for detective work. If you type "Matt Casella" into an Internet search engine, for example, you'll discover that he was not only involved in *The Mickey Mouse Club* but that he also had a hand in casting such movies as Robin Williams's *Good Morning, Vietnam* and the 1980s blockbuster hit *Flashdance.* "I've had an eclectic career," Matt says, laughing. Eclectic, yes. But *legitimate.*

Matt also recommends that you bring your child to an audition "as a blank slate visually." He explains:

"People feel their kids must look like today's pop stars—with the hair and the makeup and all that. Don't do it. Go for the natural look. Let us use our imaginations for how the kid is going to look while performing professionally.

"When I was holding auditions for The Mickey Mouse Club, *I told at least half of the kids I wanted to see again in a callback that they should return with a clean face. And sometimes I asked them to remove all makeup on the spot."*

I'll expand Matt's advice to include what your child wears on her feet. I have twelve-year-old girls come to my office wearing four-inch heels. They look seventeen. One of my regular questions upon meeting a potential client is, "How tall are you really?"

I also want to caution you against letting your child try out for one of the television talent competitions that have become all the rage. Because these are "reality" shows, the producers have to create drama—and often that means humiliating the contestants. As Matt puts it, "It's like slowing down on the road to get a look at an accident. A lot of people tune in to *American Idol* just to see what's going to come out of Simon's mouth."

One of my clients—an extremely talented singer—recently tried out for a similar show, and I will never, ever again allow any of my clients to go that route. My client called it the worst experience of her life. In the week before the show was taped, she and the other contestants were bullied and rehearsed to the point of utter exhaustion. By the time they were told whether or not they would appear on the show, all of them were completely frightened and upset. My client made the cut, but after she sang her song, one of the judges remarked, "Stick to karaoke." That snippet was used in the commercial promoting the show for the entire week before it aired. My client was devastated.

When I related that episode to Matt he told me with dismay that in the last couple of years, when he's held auditions of his own, mothers who have never met him have been approaching him with requests along the lines of "Please don't upset Tyler so much that he runs off the stage crying." Matt prides himself on the child-friendly atmosphere of his auditions and in the fact that many kids leave his office remarking, "I had fun!" Even Britney Spears has said in several interviews, "Matt is cool. He's so laid-back!"

I share Matt's philosophy: When a child leaves an audition, she should feel good about herself whether or not she got the part. She should feel good about herself *just because she did it.*

Another thing you and your child should keep in mind if she isn't chosen is that she may attract special notice and even be considered for other projects. Matt remembers an eleven- or twelve-year-old Jessica Simpson from her auditions for *The Mickey Mouse Club*: "I was really taken with her singing and her look—she resembled a young Cindy Crawford." Jessica made the finals but eventually lost out to Britney Spears and Christina Aguilera. A more immediate success story was Mayim Bialik. "I knew Mayim wasn't right for *The Mickey Mouse Club* but I suggested her for the role of the young Bette Midler in the movie *Beaches*," Matt says. "Subsequently, a sitcom was developed for her. She starred in *Blossom* for about five years."

Making a Demo

Your child will need an audio recording of herself singing in order to attract a manager, producer, or label. One of the things I'm concerned about in the music business right now is the ridiculous amounts people are spending on demos. Please be advised that early in your child's career she doesn't need a big fancy demo. These days, hopefuls are spending $300 or $400 on a three- or five-track machine to make their own demos at home and that will do just fine.

If it's financially possible, however, your child should have her own, original material. Remember: People in the business are not looking for the next Britney Spears, so it doesn't make sense to sing a Britney Spears song. For a reasonable price, you can hire a local songwriter to create a couple of original numbers. You can find such a person by doing an Internet search for "songwriters" plus the name of your city or the nearest major city. In this way you'll find organizations such as the Philadelphia Songwriters Association and the San Diego Songwriters Guild. These groups should be able to provide leads.

Be sure to get it in writing from the musician that the rights to the song will not be sold to anyone else. When producer Brian Lukow was auditioning singers for Huckapoo, he heard three different girls sing the same song. Each had been promised that the song had been written only for her, and each paid upward of $1,000 for the rights to it. "And it turned out to be a pretty crummy song," Brian says.

The Internet has a lot of good information about making a demo—more than we are able to give here. Use the search terms "how to make a demo."

Finding and Hiring the Right Professionals

As I mentioned earlier in this chapter, you work with different types of professionals in the music business from those you would in other segments of the entertainment industry. Basically, you will be working with a manager and a producer. But getting an entertainment attorney—specifically, one who is familiar with the music business—is the best place to start. There are two reasons for this. One: The attorney may be able to suggest good management and production people for your child. As manager/producer Bert Price puts it, "I haven't yet found a town with an entertainment lawyer who didn't have connections to someone in the industry." And two: The attorney will negotiate your contracts with the manager and producer and, eventually, your record label. Early in your child's career, before she is offered a deal by a label, a music attorney will typically charge you by the hour at a rate of between $175 and $350.

Where to find the right lawyer? Word of mouth is always best. You can also ask another industry professional—I get calls all the time looking for recommendations: "I've got a deal. What should I do?" Another tactic: Find out who the big names use. See which attorney names come up in industry publications such as *Billboard*. Some artists thank their lawyers by name in the liner notes to their CDs. Check your local bar association—some offer referral services. There are also reference books that provide contact information for all kinds of music industry types. One is *The Ultimate Survival Guide to the New Music Industry* by Justin Goldberg (Lone Eagle Publishing Company, 2004), which includes a CD-ROM of contact info.

Next, your child will need a manager and a producer. You can find candidates via many of the same sources I've named above. Your manager can also help you find a producer and vice versa. And sometimes industry pros will find *you*. You won't see many of them lurking at county fairs, but they do visit clubs in search of new performers. Bert Price explains the manager's role in a pop artist's career:

"Because budgets are much smaller than they are in other entertainment industry fields, you can employ fewer people, and the fewer people there are the more jobs each person has to do.

"As a manager in the music business, I have to go outside the role of the traditional manager in the entertainment field, who may just field phone calls and coordinate the relationships among the agents, lawyers, account-ants, and promoters. I also have to be a psychiatrist, a babysitter, the pro-duction company . . . and when someone breaks a tooth, I handle that, too. You have to wear so many hats in this business.

"The manager is the most important person in any artist's career, so you really have to choose carefully. You need to develop the relationship slowly,

because it's really based on trust. After all, the manager has access to everything. But that trust has to be a two-way street. A good manager isn't going to be quick to jump into a contract with you and your child, and you shouldn't be quick to jump, either."

Bert says a manager works on a commission of between 15 and 25 percent of an artist's income, and it's usually at the higher end at the beginning of the artist's career. "The percentage is often reduced when the manager recoups a certain amount of his initial investment in the group or artist," according to Bert.

A producer is in charge of bringing the **master recording**— the finished product—to the record company. Bert says there are basically two kinds of producers:

Master recording:

A recording that is ready to go to market.

"The producer can be somebody like Stevie Wonder or Teddy Riley who are literally musicians and make and play the music. Or he can be like Puff Daddy or Quincy Jones who hire the best guys in the business to do the musical part while they make the key decisions—and that is production in the more traditional sense of the word. The producer is a hands-on guy, much like the director of a movie."

He may be employed by one of the record companies or he can be independent, affiliated with his own studio, in which case he **shops** the product to record companies. Bert explains the latter:

To shop (a recording):

To present a demo recording to a number of record labels in hope that one company will want to sign that artist or group and produce a recording of the music to sell.

"This is called a production deal, and usually the producer works on a per-centage basis—he may, for example, take 40 to 60 percent of the royalties the record makes. This is the kind of deal I had with Imajin and that Johnny Wright had with *NSYNC and the Backstreet Boys."

Another member of your child's team will be an account-ant, also called a business manager. "He's in charge of paying the manager his commission and whatever else the artist tells him to pay . . . whether it's the artist's personal expenses or only those related to the record deal or record industry," Bert says, adding that the accountant can work for a percentage or by the hour.

Once your child is offered a deal by a label, the attorney comes back into the picture to negotiate the deal. At this point, Bert says, instead of working for an hourly rate the attorney usu-ally wants to take a 5 to 10 percent cut of the advance. It may seem like you are handing out a lot of "cuts"—20 percent here, 5 percent there, 5 percent to yet another person—but Bert says to keep in mind that people tend to work harder if they have some equity in the project, if they know they're going to make more money for themselves. He adds:

> *"One of the reasons it's crucial to have an experienced attorney when you negotiate your first record deal is that the label may be talking about things that mean nothing to you now but that can end up meaning a lot if you're a success. Take merchandising—who will own the right to license your child's face? In one year, the New Kids on the Block did something like a billion dollars in merchandising—on posters and so forth."*

Obviously, it pays to have a team of solid professionals backing your child.

Going It Alone

Some parents have the chutzpah to approach the **A&R (artists and repertoire)** departments of record labels on their own. Going this route is less daunting than it used to be. "It's true that most record companies still frown upon doing a deal with a minor, because they have to go through a long and expensive legal process," says Bert Price. "They have to petition the court in the child's state of residence to be able to legally make the record deal. Then there are other mitigating factors. For example, in New York, because of the Child Performer Education and Trust Act of 2003, the minor has to maintain a certain grade point average." But thanks to the wild success in recent years of labels like Jive that target a preteen and young-teen audience and feature artists who aren't much older, major players like Disney and Nickelodeon have expanded into the pop business because it's a natural fit—they were already set up to deal with minors, according to Bert. "They already had a built-in legal department to deal with all the issues and relationships with the courts and can expedite matters," he says.

A&R (artists & repertoire):

The department of a record company responsible for talent acquisition.

It stands to reason, then, that your best course of action when you're researching the market at the music store is to find the labels that are regularly recording minors. I've already mentioned a few sources of contact information. Another is a CD-ROM called *All Music Industry Contacts.* Reasonably priced, it includes contact information and credits for A&Rs, managers, producers, and music publishers (go to *www.allmusicindustrycontacts.com*).

"You have to be persistent," says *Driven* producer Beth Melillo. "You have to know who to go to and you have to bang down every door until they agree to see you."

The Rocky Road of Pop Stardom

It's a long, hard climb...but it doesn't get easier at the top. If your child makes it in the music business, here's what the two of you should expect.

Life as She Knows It Will Cease to Exist

Music stars attract very young fans, who tend to be the most exuberant, emotional, and adoring fans there are. It boggles my mind when my client John Sutherland tells me about his experiences as a member of the group B3, which is hugely popular in Europe, and especially in Germany. John, an American, says the girls just go nuts when they see him on the streets, chanting "John-nee, John-nee, John-nee!" He can't go anywhere in Germany without bodyguards. On the other hand, because the group's music hasn't been released in the United States, he is a virtual unknown in America, and can go anywhere he wants to here without hassle. It's a strange double life, but John admits that it's a relief to come home!

Most pop stars, of course, aren't so lucky. If your child becomes a star in the United States, she will no longer be able to go to the mall on a whim. She'll need to completely disguise herself to avoid being mobbed. She'll find that people will be watching her every move—and often those people are photographers. She won't even be able to dash into the supermarket for a carton of milk without looking her best lest she find her picture splashed across a tabloid in an "Ew! Stars Without Style!" feature. Celebrity is particularly hard on teens because in our culture adolescence has been designed for spontaneity, for bonding with friends, for having fun, for acting silly at times.

Adolescence is also the time of life in which humans experience dramatic physical and emotional changes and therefore are hardest on themselves about their looks. This makes typical teens extremely vulnerable when criticized about their bodies. Multiply this exponentially for pop stars because they are the targets of countless more sources of criticism. Tabloids are either jeering at them for gaining weight or accusing them of having an eating disorder such as anorexia or bulimia. While these disorders are already a big problem in the general teen and young adult populations, the pressure to remain thin in the entertainment industry is so intense that these disorders are even more common, unfortunately.

Your family may have to move—and take other precautions—for security reasons or simply because the work is elsewhere. For example, all of the kids selected for *The Mickey Mouse Club*—and at least one family member each—had to move to Orlando,

Florida, because the Mouseketeers primarily worked at Walt Disney World.

Your child may have to grow up sooner than he or she is ready to. I know of sixteen- and seventeen-year-old boys in popular music groups who were stunned—and even a bit frightened—at the blatant way female fans threw themselves at them sexually. I also need not elaborate on the fact that drug and alcohol abuse has haunted the music industry for decades.

Your Child May Have to Play a Part Instead of Just Being Herself

I have already made it clear that pop groups are often cast—that is, the producer has a concept and is looking for performers to play certain roles . . . say, one "sporty" type, one "posh" type, one "sexy" type. This has been going on since the early days of pop, with the advent of the Monkees. Mickey Dolenz was supposed to be the "crazy" one, Mike Nesmith the "quiet, studious" one, and so forth. Still, typecasting is much more prevalent today, and your child may be pressured to play her role whenever she's in public, not just while performing.

This happens with solo performers as well. A pop star's handlers, the media, and sometimes even her fans create a persona that may in no way resemble her true self. It can be difficult and disheartening to live up to the image. The celebrity media often describe Britney Spears as a "pop tart," and I have heard and read parents complaining that she's a bad influence on young girls. Well, I liken what Britney Spears became to a Barbie doll—what you see isn't real. Most of the public has no idea how shy Britney really is. In fact, Matt Casella says that when both Britney and Christina Aguilera came to audition for him, they were so painfully shy in their initial interviews—where he asks kids ice-

breaking questions such as "What are your favorite subjects at
school?"—he almost didn't let them perform for him! "When
they did sing," Matt says, "it was like they'd flipped on a switch
inside. They just shined."

Your Child May Have to Perform
Songs or Make Statements That Don't
Reflect Her Own Values

This is a natural consequence of the phenomenon we just discussed. Sex sells, as we all know, and so do songs about various
forms of partying. Depending on the mood of the country, your
child may even be pressured to take a political stance that isn't
her own. The flip side of this is that she may be discouraged
from singing or talking about the things that she does believe in.
Matt Casella says Christina Aguilera is one of the few pop stars
who "speaks her own mind and who is her own person. Early
on, she stood behind causes like AIDS and women's shelters."
More recently, in "Beautiful," Christina wrote and sang about
how "you are beautiful no matter what they say"—a lone, com-
forting voice for teenage girls who are constantly bombarded by
advertisements, the media, and their peers with the opposite
message.

Your Child May Be This Month's
Flavor—and Next Year's Nobody

Most of us know of pop groups that were sensations in the
1980s or 1990s . . . and then seemingly disappeared from the face
of the earth, their members neither seen nor heard from since.
Bert Price has watched this happen time after time. "It's hard for
a bunch of guys who have just now sort of come into their own at
nineteen or twenty, who have finally grown up, and they're back at
ground zero after traveling the world with a hit record," he says.

"The fact is that while kids break into this business because they're cute, you can't bank on being cute forever. What's going to happen when you pass puberty and you're not as cute anymore? As a parent, you really have to consider this when you put your kid into show business."

Bert says that the members of the groups he's handled don't suffer such devastating crashes because he will only work with kids who are not just cute but also talented. Just as important, he constantly encourages them to keep developing as musicians and performers, to work on getting better and better no matter how famous they are so that when the time comes they can make the transition from teen pop idol to serious and respected adult singer or musician. "I tell my guys to look at actors Leonardo DiCaprio and Johnny Depp, both of whom got their first breaks because they had cute faces," Bert says. "They had acting talent, but they didn't stop developing as actors. They worked at perfecting their craft. And today as adults they are considered immensely talented actors and have their pick of roles." Johnny Depp, in fact, is often described as his generation's Marlon Brando.

Their counterparts in the pop world are veterans Cher and Madonna. Not only are these women—one in her late forties and one in her late fifties—still making millions and *People* magazine, they are constantly acquiring new skills *and* branching out into other forms of music and media. Madonna is even writing children's books these days. They have reinvented themselves time and time again, not just to keep up with current trends, but to *launch* trends as well.

Bottom line: Don't ever stop encouraging your child to grow.

Making It in the Music Scene—NOTES

- The music business is the most difficult in the entertainment field to break into and the most difficult in which to sustain a career.
- It isn't as regulated as other segments of the entertainment industry.
- Pop music performers and their parents have to make many sacrifices, and the biggest of these is time.
- Young pop stars have three things in common: talent, desire, and the right parent(s).
- Career preparation involves lessons, experience, exposure, and lots of auditioning.

8

Putting Together a Support Team

Show business, whatever else it might be, is a business, one with many complexities and gray areas. Proper handling of your child's business affairs is ultimately your responsibility, but you're also going to need the help and advice of a team of business specialists. In this chapter we'll look at some important financial and legal issues that pertain to children in show business. I also give you tips on when and how to work with accountants, lawyers, and publicists—experts for hire who can help further your child's career.

Publicity usually is not an important consideration until a child is well established. Therefore, we will talk about working with publicists in the final section of this chapter. Accountants and lawyers, on the other hand, are professionals whose services you will need early on. I suggest that you line up a qualified accountant and attorney as soon as possible—certainly before your child receives his first professional check or signs his first contract.

Finding the Right Accountant

This will require some effort on your part. As you may recall from our discussion about finding representation, I believe in shopping around before committing to working with someone. It's most important that you select people with whom you are comfortable, and that you hire experts—professionals with lots of show business experience. Try to get several referrals from agents, managers, acquaintances in the business, or your local accountant. Be sure to interview at least two or three before making a decision.

I remember that as soon as my daughter, Bonnie, started working, the accountant who had long handled my family's finances told me, "I can try to feel my way through this. But frankly, you are dealing in a specialized and confusing area of accounting. You'd be much better off finding someone with experience in show business. Let me give you a few referrals." I didn't know it then, but that accountant was doing me an enormous favor. The finances of launching Bonnie's show business career were almost as complex as those of starting my own business, so I really did need a specialist.

As your child becomes successful in his performing career, your financial responsibilities increase. You may not realize it, but as a parent, you are legally responsible for the proper handling of your child's money. If, when your child comes of age, he feels that you haven't managed his money in a competent and reasonable manner, he can take you to court and ask to be reimbursed.

"I always tell parents not to do anything with their child's money that they wouldn't do with their own," says Marvin Katz, a New York–based accountant who handles a variety of show business clients. "If you do

anything out of the ordinary, you had better be able to demonstrate that you are doing it for the child's sake, not your own.

"For example, if you buy a new house with your son's money and his name isn't on the title, you may have a big problem down the road. When that child becomes an adult, he can sue you and ask you to demonstrate that what you did was reasonable and in his best interests. That's why it's important to keep records and document all your expenses from the very beginning, and why it's necessary to have the help and guidance of a skilled professional."

When shopping for an accountant, you will find that many will be willing to talk to you on the phone, and some will agree to meet you in person. Be sure to ask in advance if you will be charged for this initial interview. If the answer is yes, you also had better ask if you'll be billed each time you call up with a question. Every professional has his or her own way of working. Accountant Marvin Katz deals with each situation on an individual basis.

"Normally, prospective clients talk to me on the phone. However, if it's not during tax season, I will usually sit and talk with people about their financial picture without charge. If it is during tax season, my approach depends on the kind of questions a person wants to ask. My time is money. I may tell you that there is a fee—payable in advance—to talk to me in person.

"When someone is willing to pay for an hour of time, that indicates that she is really interested in doing business with me, not just looking for free advice. Once we've established a relationship, I don't run a meter. I know how much time the average person doing commercials is going to need, and I set my fee on that basis. Fifteen or twenty minutes more or less isn't going to make a difference."

As your child's career progresses, you may find it to your advantage to let that same accountant handle all of your family's financial affairs. But this depends on a number of factors, such as how much money your child is making relative to your family's total income. The financial relationship between a child performer and her parents is a delicate one. Therefore, the accountant must have a thorough understanding of a family's entire financial picture.

Naturally, the fees your accountant charges will be based, to a large extent, on how many hours he spends working for you and how complicated your situation is.

"Everybody puts a price on his own talent," says Katz. "I'll charge some clients $100 an hour for tax work, and I'll charge other clients $350 an hour for tax work. It depends on my relationship with the person and on his or her potential to make money. I'll sometimes lower my fee if a person has potential but isn't making a lot yet."

In almost every instance the difference in fees between a specialist and your family accountant is far less than what you can save at tax time. For example, there are many deductions performers can legally take, many of which are not spelled out in any IRS guidelines (see page 181). An accountant with show business experience has a much better sense of what is—or is not—a safe deduction in a given year.

Also, if you are challenged by the IRS about a particular deduction, a specialist will be more knowledgeable about precedents, and therefore more likely to persuade the auditor to retain that deduction.

Finding the Right Attorney

This is very similar to finding a good accountant. There are, however, several important differences in how you work with these professionals. Unlike accountants, entertainment lawyers typically do not become involved with any other aspect of your family's legal interests. And while you probably won't need a specialized accountant until your child starts earning money, it may be necessary to retain the services of an entertainment attorney before your child actually works professionaly.

I've seen parents sign horrendous contracts with local agents and managers. These one-sided, but perfectly legal, documents tie children up for years and sometimes ruin their careers. That's why you should consult a qualified entertainment attorney whenever your child is asked to enter into a contractual agreement.

Keep in mind that attorneys who are perfectly competent to do general legal work often have no idea how to negotiate a show business contract. The price of a good entertainment lawyer in New York or Los Angeles currently averages between $250 to $450 per hour—definitely not cheap. Still, that really isn't such a high price when measured against your child's professional future.

In shopping for an attorney, you are likely to be treated better if you come referred by someone he knows. If you don't have any contacts in show business, you can ask attorneys in other fields for referrals. As with doctors, lawyers are often able to recommend qualified specialists. Be sure to ask about the credentials of the lawyer being recommended—what types of clients she represents, how many years of experience she has, and what her fees are going to be. If you can't find a referral, you can call the New York or Los Angeles bar associations and ask them for a list of members who belong to their entertainment sections. If you want an entertainment lawyer closer to home, you can call the nearest large metropolitan area or state bar association.

"If you're really serious about helping your child succeed in show business, don't waste your time dealing with lawyers outside of the major media centers," advises one Los Angeles entertainment attorney. "There are many good local attorneys, but the reality is that you need professionals who are located where the major show business action is. If you're a Midwesterner and your child is interested in modeling, I can see the point of hiring a lawyer in Chicago. If you're a musical performer, it might make sense to have a lawyer in Detroit or Nashville, cities where the music industry is big. But if you want your child to be on national TV, in the movies, or on Broadway, you need an entertainment lawyer who is New York— or Los Angeles—based."

Be aware that many entertainment attorneys in the major show business cities perform functions not generally associated with their colleagues in other fields—functions that sometimes overlap with those of agents and managers. A good lawyer can be one of your most important contacts in the business.

"I will meet with a family for an initial conversation to get to know what it is that they are after," says L.A. entertainment lawyer Frank Lunn. "I find if I'm a good listener, then I can get to the heart of the matter. I usually don't charge for this initial meeting. If we go on to have subsequent meetings, then I will charge for my time."

If you are completely new to the business and unsigned to a manager or an agent, it is certainly worthwhile to sit down with an entertainment attorney for one hour and let him give you some idea about the laws in your local state and what kind of contracts he would want you to consider. You may also have a list of possible agents, and he may suggest and even refer you to three or four of them. Buying an hour of time with an attorney is a straight-ahead deal. He isn't going to tell you that your child can be a star and ask you to sign a contract, and he isn't going to try to sell you services that you don't need.

You can generally interview attorneys on the phone free of charge, as long as you are talking about their qualifications and fees. Once you start discussing your specific goals and asking for their business and legal advice, however, you can expect the meter to start running. Some attorneys will not grant a free initial in-person interview. They feel that they are entitled to be compensated for every hour of their time. But there are other attorneys who will not charge to meet with you and explore how you can work together.

The way any given attorney works depends on the status and inclination of that particular person, the policy of his law firm, and the quality of your referral. Mark Sendroff, a New York entertainment attorney, has a flexible approach to the issue of charging for an initial consultation:

"I'm interviewed all the time by people shopping for an attorney. When someone calls me up and says, 'I'm interested in finding a lawyer—how much will you charge?' I say, 'I'll charge you a flat fee for a one-hour consultation, or I'll charge you nothing if you're just interviewing me for fif-teen minutes to see if we're compatible.' I think people have a right to meet me without being charged, as long as they don't ask me specific legal ques-

tions. I must admit, though, that I sometimes have a hard time completely avoiding those questions."

Mothers and fathers seem to have several basic problems in working with attorneys: either they are scared to use one because they think the costs will be prohibitive, or they are worried that the lawyer might advise them not to sign, and that's not what they want to hear. On the other hand, I've also come across parents who run to a lawyer every time they have a question about a comma or a period. Once you establish a good working relationship with an attorney, he should be able to help you find a sensible middle ground. If you have limited funds, make that clear at the beginning. Most lawyers will work out some kind of payment plan that fits in with your budget.

"I try to make an arrangement that makes sense to a client," says Frank Lunn. "I can structure a deal whereby the manager or agent negotiates the basic deal points and then I clean up the contract and finish the negotiations for a straight five percent of the deal. If at some point the manager or agent does not represent the client anymore, then I charge a flat ten percent."

Until your child becomes relatively successful, there is usually no reason to run up thousands of dollars in legal fees. The most important thing is to have someone you can turn to when you need him. Utilize your attorney's services selectively, but don't ever completely ignore his advice or try to make complex legal decisions on your own.

"The child actor definitely needs a good team that includes an agent and/or manager and an attorney," advises Frank Lunn. "A lot of times parents are not familiar with the roles that each of us plays. My job as an attorney is not to get your name around town; my job is to protect your interests. It's the agent or manager's job to get your name out.

"What I do when I'm brought into a situation is to make sure that I have a good working relationship with the agent or manager. It is really a team effort. If we have that relationship and the client has a deal on the table, then I can be brought in on the early stages to handle the agreement so that the client realizes the best possible deal.

"I think in the case of a child, the best and most cost-effective scenario is having an agent who can find work and negotiate the deal points, and an attorney who can protect the rights of the child. This works particularly well if you find an agent who is willing to do the hand-holding, which some managers are also great at."

Understanding the Legal End of Show Business

Although you ultimately will need your lawyer to interpret the language of a contract, it's important that you understand the key issues that are involved. In fact, the more you know about what you are signing, the better your attorney will be able to guide you and negotiate on your child's behalf.

Since there are no federal laws governing children working in the entertainment industry, you should first be aware of the state laws governing the employment hours of children in the entertainment field, the **work permits** that are required, and the laws pertaining to schooling while your child is on the job. These laws vary greatly, but I think it's fair to say that California has the strictest and most comprehensive set of legal guidelines involving young performers, and New York's new law is not far behind.

Work permit:

A legal document issued by a city or state giving a child permission to work.

You can obtain information by contacting your state Department of Labor, Employment Standards Division, or Department of Social Services, or the SAG, AFTRA, or Equity office nearest you.

Once you are aware of the laws of your state, you should have a working knowledge of the various contracts your child may be asked to enter into. Show business contracts can be divided into two broad categories: those that are regulated by one of the unions, and those that are not subject to union regulation. In general, if a **franchised agent** gives you a standard union contract with no alterations or additions, you are safe. These contracts are designed by the unions to protect both affiliated performers and agents. If your child is not a union member and you want to see a standard agency contract, you can write to the unions and request copies.

Franchised agent:

An agent who agrees to follow the rules and guidelines set by AEA, SAG, and/or AFTRA in the representation of his clients, and who has been approved by these unions.

In a standard SAG or Equity contract the agent cannot take more than a 10 percent commission, and the term of the initial agreement is limited to one year. Therefore, after that first year, both you and the agent are free to make a decision about whether or not you want to continue the relationship. If you do decide to re-sign, subsequent contracts can extend for longer periods.

Union agency contracts have an **out clause** that allows you to automatically terminate the contract if the agent hasn't found work for your child within ninety-one days. Parents who trust their agents often won't exercise this option because they understand that agents only line up the auditions; performers actually get the work. Still, it's a comfortable feeling to have this kind of protection written into your contract. As I mentioned in chapter 5, there are three major unions that franchise agents: SAG (Screen Actors Guild), AFTRA (American Federation of Television and Radio Artists), and AEA (Actors' Equity Association). Each of these unions is separate and independent from the others (although SAG and AFTRA are on the verge of merging). Each has its own entrance requirements, initiation fees, and annual dues. Let's briefly review the three major performing arts unions and the kinds of work each one covers.

Out clause:

The part of a legal contract that defines the conditions under which a performer may terminate the agreement.

AFTRA has jurisdiction over actors, singers, dancers, recording artists, or anyone employed in television shows and commercials that are live or recorded on audio or videotape. It also covers all other performers in television and radio, including announcers, news reporters, and disc jockeys.

SAG has jurisdiction over actors appearing in motion pictures, television shows, and commercials that are recorded on film. The motion pictures and commercials may be shown in either movie theaters or on television.

AEA has jurisdiction over actors and stage managers in live theater or industrial shows.

A performer does not have to join any of the unions to work nonunion jobs. After your child accepts her first union job, she may continue to work for thirty days without becoming a union member. However, she must join the appropriate union if she stays on the job longer than that, or is hired for her second union job after the thirty-day period. Once a performer does join a union, she is usually forbidden to accept any nonunion employment.

You can find more information about contacting and joining SAG, AFTRA, and Equity in the Appendix. Keep in mind that all three unions frequently amend their bylaws, so be sure to ask for the most current rules when you request information.*

Since the performing arts unions exist primarily to protect the interests of their members, their standard contracts are designed with that purpose in mind. Still, it would be wise to call the unions before signing with an agent to make sure that the agent's franchise is in good standing. Be sure to check with your lawyer to verify that you are indeed signing a standard union contract. Also keep in mind that you are not locked into the minimum standards set by the unions. As attorney Frank Lunn points out, "Nothing prevents you from negotiating terms that are more in your favor than the standards set by the union. There may be points in an agent or manager's

---

*As of November 2004, the franchise agreement between agents and SAG has expired, and a new agreement has not yet been approved by SAG membership. In the interim most agents are signing actors to a General Service Agreement written jointly by ATA (Association of Talent Agents) and NATR (National Association of Talent Representatives), the east and west coast organizations for theatrical agents. This agreement incorporates most of the rules of the SAG franchise agreement. SAG is currently considering actors signed to the General Service Agreement as being validly signed to an agency. This is no way affects Equity and AFTRA agency franchises.

contract that are simply nonnegotiable. I can look at the contract, however, and let the family know what it is that they are getting into."

Since managers are not franchised by the unions or licensed by any governmental or other regulating authority, they can ask for whatever terms you are willing to accept. And because there are no minimum standards, management contracts have to be carefully examined and evaluated by your attorney. Although the specific legal questions are far too numerous and complex for us to discuss in this chapter, I think it's important for parents to be able to answer the following key questions before signing any contract:

What Is the Length of the Agreement?

I have always felt that a contract is just a piece of paper. Real commitments come from the satisfaction of both parties. If a performer is happy with his representative, he won't want to get out of his contract. By the same token, I would never want to hold somebody who doesn't want me to represent him—no matter what the terms of a contract. Still, for your own protection, there should be a reasonable, mutually acceptable limit on the length of any agreement.

"Managers can sometimes help young performers at the early stages of their careers," says one attorney. "As part of the compensation for that service, managers will usually ask that a child be under contract for an extended period of time. In some cases, the child may start doing well through his own efforts. But if the management contract is still in effect, the manager will continue to take his percentage."

Parents who find themselves in this type of situation sometimes try to take legal action against the manager, claiming that he didn't fulfill his part of the contract. I think that if you are going to sign with a manager, your best protection is to sign with someone who is legitimate and trustworthy. Determining a person's good faith before you enter into a contract is a lot better than trying to take him to court after you've signed.

Options are renewal clauses in a contract that determine the actual length of time you are represented. When you sign a contract, you need to be aware of what the entire term adds up to. Watch out for clauses that automatically extend the agreement without your approval, or you can tie up your child with one manager for years. When you sign a three-year management agreement with a two-year option on the manager's part, for example, you are actually making a five-year commitment. However, if the options are mutual, the term of the contract cannot be extended without your consent. An experienced attorney can phrase the contract to protect the performer as well as the manager.

Options:
Specific conditions under which points, rights, or services are renewable.

Perhaps the best protection a parent can have in signing a management contract is to base renewal options on the manager's fulfillment of specific requirements. If you sign a three-year agreement, for example, you can add a clause stating that if your child has not earned a certain amount of money during a predetermined period of time, you have the right to terminate the contract. Renewals can also be based on things other than money. The important point here is that you require a manager to produce concrete results for your child before he can exercise his option to renew the contract. What you are doing, in essence, is tying the length of the contract to the manager's performance.

Which Work Will Be Commissioned?

Before you enter into a contract with a representative, you should be fully aware of any and all rights that you are signing away. Some management contracts call for a commission on all work your child might do in the creative and performing arts. Such clauses may not seem important when you first sign, but they can become very significant as time goes on and your child discovers that she has other viable talents. In asking for a percentage of monies that a child might earn in other show-business–related fields, a manager might claim that his advice and counsel helped open doors in those areas—and he might have a point. It is important to establish exactly in which creative and performing areas a manager is prepared and qualified to provide service.

"When parents are meeting with a manager, agent, or attorney," notes entertainment lawyer Frank Lunn, "they should make sure they feel very comfortable with the person, that they are aware of the obligations that they are creating, and that they understand what is expected of them in that relationship. They should ask, 'What is this person going to do to further my child's career?' They should also ask for names of people who can provide recommendations for that person, to see the level of respect that person has within the industry. The better informed they are as parents, the better they are going to be able to help their child in the industry.

"There needs to be a lot of honesty back and forth, a lot of integrity, and the feeling of, 'Let's grow together in this relationship' rather than, 'I'm going to use you and see what I can get out of you.' I'm really big on the team concept. Don't accept the first person that you talk to on the telephone. Take the time and effort to form the right team for you."

A related issue to be aware of is that the money a child makes due to the efforts of an agent or manager is often commission-able by that representative after the **term of the contract** is up. When a franchised agent books a child on a TV series, for example, she will continue to collect her commission on the **residuals** that client collects from **reruns** five or ten years later, even if the client is no longer with that agency. Management contracts usually contain similar clauses—and justifiably so. But here again, there is nothing that prevents a manager from asking for a commission on work that your child obtained without his help or expertise.

Term of contract:
The length of time for which a contract is in effect.

Residuals:
Fees paid to a performer for the rebroadcast of a TV show, film, or commercial in which the performer appears.

Reruns:
The rebroadcast of a TV show, film, or commercial.

How Much Power Are You Giving Away?
Managers often ask their clients to give them **power of attor-ney.** This pertains to the power a manager has to make decisions on your child's behalf—financial or otherwise—without con-sulting you. For example, some contracts give a manager the right to collect and endorse checks, to sign contracts, and to approve publicity. Giving your manager power of attorney can

help make him more effective in representing you. But because it is an expression of confidence and good faith on your part, it should not be given lightly, and you should consult with an attorney first.

Power of attorney:

The authorizing of another to act as one's agent or attorney, empowering him or her with specific rights—such as signing checks, making commitments, etc.

Whatever kind of power you might give a representative, make certain that you retain the right to pull your child out of the business completely—if that's what you want to do. I've seen highly talented youngsters suddenly decide that they no longer had any interest in performing. If that day should ever come, there should be nothing in a contract that permits anyone to compel your child to continue.

"I would be extremely careful in granting a manager power of attorney if I were a parent," advises attorney Mark Sendroff. "Unless you really know and trust a manager, I wouldn't let him endorse and cash any of my child's income checks. I also would not permit the manager to accept work or enter into any other kind of binding agreement without my approval.

"Some managers ask for the authority to endorse products on behalf of a child. That kind of thing means money to a manager, and, after all, they are in this to make their percentage. Parents should think twice before granting this kind of power to a manager, because some product endorsements are not beneficial to a young performer's image. Parents have to determine why a manager wants a particular power of attorney and just how he plans to use it."

How Much Money Are You Giving Away?

As we've seen, the unions typically limit a franchised agent's commissions to 10 percent. When your child signs an exclusive agency agreement, that commission applies not only to employment found by the agent, but also to any performing work secured by your child. In most cases, if a child signs with me and then books something locally on her own, I'll say, "Don't worry about it—you don't owe me on this one." On the other hand, I become upset when clients try to accept work without my knowledge. Here again, I think the key to resolving any particular situation rests with the quality of the relationship you have with your agent. I must admit that I am prone to try harder for those clients whose parents treat me with consideration.

Trust and respect are no less important in your relationships with managers. Nevertheless, their commission structures have to be very carefully scrutinized. Most reputable show business managers charge between 10 and 20 percent. "If a manager wants to charge anything more than 25 percent," advises one entertainment attorney, "I would consider that a red flag."

If you do decide to sign with a manager, there are a number of important financial questions to consider, aside from the percentage you are paying. With franchised agents, most financial matters are regulated by the unions. Since managers don't have such restrictions, they can write all sorts of questionable, but absolutely legal, clauses into contracts. Let me give you two cases in point.

I know several managers who deduct their expenses every time they come to see certain young clients perform. Of course, people can negotiate any kind of contract they want. But personally I can't find much justification for a manager taking this kind of commission. My feeling is that unless the manager accompanies your child to a job at your request, you shouldn't have to foot his bills.

I recently ran into one mother who was upset because she realized that she had signed a management contract that permitted her daughter's manager to collect commissions on her expense money. I shared her outrage. Expense money is given to a performer to cover only his expenses—it is not a fee earned by a child. Therefore, I would never sign an agreement permitting a manager to take a commission on that.

In spite of the problems that come up in negotiating management agreements, I know many parents who are extremely happy with their children's managers. Again, in deciding whether to sign with any representative, you first have to make sure he is ethical and then measure the potential value of his services against what they are going to cost.

Before we move on to a discussion of managing the finances of your child's career, I'd like to discuss an important but frequently overlooked aspect of contracts involving minors. Unless a child's contract is court-approved, it can be broken on the grounds of "infancy" in *many* states even if it is signed by the parent. Essentially, that allows a minor to get out of a contract because of his age. Most managers and agents don't seek court approval beforehand; it is generally a very long and costly process. Therefore, in many situations a child could actually get out of a contract at any time.

This law would seem to put representatives in a vulnerable position, but one lawyer told me that this is as it should be: "I think that the notion of having a court approve a minor's contract is terrific because it protects the welfare of young people. Let's remember that we're talking about children who are not yet ready to make their own business decisions. As far as I'm concerned, the rights of children should transcend all business considerations. If an agent or manager doesn't want to take the time to get the contract court-approved, that's his or her problem. Somebody has to protect children from all of us, and maybe the best person to do that is a state judge."

Understanding the Financial
End of Show Business

We've seen how important it is for parents to approach show business like any other activity in which a child might develop an interest. However, this rule of thumb does not necessarily apply to
money matters. You can't know from the outset how much money
your child will earn as a professional performer. If your son
or daughter never makes any money, you can simply consider
the whole venture as another hobby. But what happens if your
child's career takes off and he starts earning a substantial income—
perhaps even more than his parents?

To be on the safe side, I suggest that you prepare yourself to
deal with both ends of the financial spectrum. In chapter 2, I
talked about how you can keep expenses down at the beginning.
Let's look at three crucial steps you can take to safeguard your
finances and those of your child.

Save All Your Receipts from Day One

Until your child begins to work, he is not considered a professional, nor are his expenses considered business-related. However,
once your child does start earning money, you are entitled to be
reimbursed for all expenses that you advanced to help launch his
career. That money would, in turn, then be deductible as expenses
from the child's taxable income.

*"Parents owe it to themselves to keep good records from the start," says
Dallas Johann, an accountant who is also the father of former child actor
Cameron Johann. "You've got start-up costs and expenses that you have to
lay out before your child can earn any income. If you don't keep accurate*

records from the very beginning, both you and your child may wind up los-
ing money. The year will go by, and if your child unexpectedly makes a lot
of money, you won't be able to deduct those expenses from his income. As a
result, you won't get reimbursed for what you laid out and he'll be in a
much higher tax bracket."

As long as your child hasn't earned any money, you don't have to file a tax return for him. But as soon as he receives his first pay-check, you can start reimbursing yourself. Here is a partial listing of expenses the IRS allows performers to deduct:

- Travel for child and adult guardian (while seeking work)
- Lodging (while seeking work)
- Meals and entertainment (while working)
- Pictures
- Résumés
- Sheet music
- Lessons
- Telephone calls
- Postage
- Accountant and lawyer fees
- Agent and manager commissions
- Business-related equipment
- Union dues
- Trade publications
- Clothing (for professional use only)
- Cosmetics
- Cost of caregiver to accompany child

There are many other expenses "Uncle Sam" will allow. How-ever, there is no official list of acceptable deductions, nor is there any guarantee that a seemingly safe and legitimate expense will not be questioned. Clothing is one of the deductions the IRS has scrutinized in recent years. One accountant whose clients include music superstars cautions that, "For an item of clothing to be deductible it must be considered a costume. That means it can't be worn as regular street clothes. If a young boy needed to buy a blue suit for an audition, for example, that would not be allowed since that suit could also be worn on the street. Whether or not the boy would actually wear it in nonprofessional situations is, of course, irrelevant."

To make certain that you receive the maximum tax benefits, I advise you to immediately begin keeping receipts for any and all expenses that you think may relate to your child generating income as a performer. But remember: as soon as your son or daughter actually starts earning money, you will need the guidance and expertise of an accountant with show business experience. Once you sit down with that accountant, it's possible—even probable—that he will throw out some of your receipts. But that's a lot better than finding out too late that because you haven't kept an ongoing record of your expenses, you can't be reimbursed for money you laid out.

Establish a Clear-Cut Business Relationship Between You and Your Child

Before your child begins earning money as a performer, you should try to set up an appropriate financial relationship between the two of you. Some mothers and fathers consider the money they invest to help their child get started a gift and have no interest in being reimbursed. Other parents consider that money a loan—to be paid back when the child begins to work.

You are required by law in New York and California to set up a blocked trust account in the child's name. Fifteen percent of your child's gross income will be deducted from his paycheck each time he works and placed in that account. This will be made available to your child when he turns eighteen. You will not be able to touch those funds without permission from the court.

In most respects, a working child is viewed exactly the same as an adult, both by his employers and by the government. Like an adult, a child must have a Social Security number before he can get paid. If a child has been working long enough to qualify, he is also entitled to unemployment insurance in some states. "In terms of salary and working conditions," accountant Marvin Katz observes, "a seven-year-old is basically no different from a forty-year-old except that there are more laws that protect the seven-year-old."

From a tax standpoint a child performer is also very much like any other business entity. "Children have to pay taxes on the income they earn," Katz points out. "A working child has his own separate identity and has to file income taxes separately from his parents. Furthermore, if the parents are not contributing more than fifty percent of what it costs to support that child, they can't declare him as a dependent."

The major difference in dealing with the finances of working children involves the way they are initially set up as businesses. If you were going into business for yourself, you could deduct your initial expenses from your taxable income. But when you help launch your child as a business, you can't deduct those expenses because the IRS views your investment as a loan. Once the child starts earning money, he can pay you back for your expenses. He can also pay you a salary for services rendered. "There are any number of ways to set up this kind of relationship," says Katz. It depends a great deal on the child's income relative to that of the parents. Katz continues:

"In general, here's how it works: The parent advances money for the child to go into show business. That money is a loan, and it's not a tax deduction

for the parent. When the child makes money he reimburses his mother for those expenses and deducts it on his tax return. Thus, when the mother lays out a dollar for the child's cab fare to an audition, it is a loan to the child. When the dollar is reimbursed by the child to the mother, it is a repayment of that loan.

"Now, let's say the child starts to make more money and begins to pay his mother ten dollars an hour for chaperoning him to jobs and auditions. At that point the mother becomes an employee of the child and the ten dollars is income to her. The child deducts it as an expense on his tax return, and the mother must, in turn, report it as income on her tax return. A professional show business child is in business, regardless of his age. Once he hires another person to render him services—be it his mother or a college student— that person owes income taxes on the money she is paid."

When a child's career starts to take off, parents will sometimes leave their jobs to be with the child and look after his interests. In some cases a parent will actually become her child's manager and take a commission. Other parents simply take a weekly or per-hour salary as compensation for their time. Here again, you have to sit down with your accountant and work out the best arrangement for your family.

Don't Forget: You Are Responsible

As the parent of a young professional performer, you have a dual role in protecting your child's interests. As the child's legal guardian, it is up to you to look after his physical and emotional welfare. And since you are also the executor of your child's assets, you have a legal obligation to protect those assets.

As we've seen, once a professional child comes of age (eighteen in most states), he can ask his parents to account for the money that he has earned. If a parent charges her child $50 an hour for accompanying him to auditions, for example, and the child can later prove that the real value of those services was only $10 an hour, the child will almost always prevail in court. That's why it's so important to be absolutely scrupulous in handling your child's money and to keep accurate records.

Bear in mind that even if your intentions are completely honorable, you can still be held accountable for not managing your child's money with a reasonable degree of competence. For example, the court might rule that a parent wasn't doing her duty if she kept most of her child's money in a regular checking account. "Your child's money should be earning interest, dividends, or capital appreciation," says Marvin Katz. "But on the other hand, the worst thing you can do is speculate with your child's money." He elaborates:

"A parent can make a speculative investment for herself, but she had better be far more conservative when she invests for the child. I tend to be over-cautious when I advise parents in this regard, because I hate to see people do things that can come back to haunt them later on."

One step you can take to avoid financial and legal complications down the road is to keep all the money your child earns in separate accounts in his name. Most families I know set the child up with his own savings account, checking account, and investments. The child always gets paid directly, and the parent should then deposit the checks into the child's bank account.

"Parents should never mingle their monies with those of the child," advises Katz. "Even if a family is very poor, they have no legal right to spend the child's

earnings. If the mother and father do use that money to support the rest of the family, the child can turn around and sue his parents when he comes of age."

I must admit that I have seen parents who go into this primarily to exploit their child's moneymaking potential. But what I come across far more often are mothers and fathers who don't even bother reimbursing themselves for the expenses they've incurred. I don't think parents should have to work at a loss once the child starts earning money, though I can understand why a financially comfortable family might prefer to leave that money with the child. The details of how you handle your child's finances will have to be worked out with your accountant and attorney. In any case, you should remember that you are responsible for the proper handling of your child's money.

Publicity and Publicists

As I mentioned at the beginning of this chapter, most young performers don't need publicity until they are well established in their careers. Even then, the potential benefits of publicity frequently don't justify the costs involved.

The great majority of my successful clients do not have a **publicist**—nor do they need one. Before we talk about when you should consider hiring a publicist for your son or daughter, I want to make sure you understand exactly what these professionals do.

Publicist (press agent):
A professional who promotes the public image of his or her clients.

"The job of a publicist is to get the word out on a person or project that requires media attention," says Patricia Story, a New York publicist who specializes in the entertainment field. *"We're professionals who work on your behalf with the media. Most high-profile celebrities have publicists on their team. There are basically two ways to do publicity: taking someone who is already visible and enhancing that publicity, or spending a lot of time, energy, and money creating exposure for someone who is unknown. In general, this approach is not effective for young performers. There is no way a publicist can make an unknown performer a star."*

I know parents who have hired local publicists, hoping to attract the attention of agents and managers. To my mind, that's putting the cart before the horse. In order for a performer to benefit from publicity, he should be already working and in the public eye. Beyond that, he should probably have a memorable role in a major film, on TV, or on Broadway before acquiring the services of a big publicist.

"A parent should consider hiring a publicist once the child has a project that has a profile high enough that it would be of interest to the media," explains Story. *"There's got to be something that the press would be interested in writing about before a publicist can approach them. Once a child has attained some kind of visibility, a good publicist can keep that momentum going. Any publicist who tells a parent that he can make an unknown child a star is not being honest. On the other hand, if a child is truly unique and special—and has done something marvelous like a **running part** on a TV series or a strong role in a movie or Broadway show—a good publicist can build on that."*

Running part:
A recurring role in a television series.

I think it's important to stress that many children who work on hit shows or films do not need a publicist. For example, if your child lands a job as one of the orphans in *Annie*, publicity would not be appropriate. The show might get a tremendous amount of media attention, but that's not the critical point here. The question you need to ask yourself is this: Is my child's role and/or performance special enough to attract significant media attention? Frankly, your agent or manager might be in a better position to offer a more objective answer to that question.

Finding a Publicist

Should you decide that the time is right to hire a publicist, ask your child's agent or manager to refer you to some qualified people. You should then interview each publicist. Ask them who they represent, and try to get a feel for their personal styles. It may not be necessary to have a publicist who represents lots of young performers. However, you should choose a specialist in the entertainment field, preferably one who has experience doing multimedia publicity for celebrities.

"I would talk to three or four different publicists to see what their style is and to see if you are comfortable with them and they are comfortable with you," says Patricia Story. "Check into their backgrounds to make sure that they have the expertise and the contacts to take your child to the media and present him in a way that will put his role in the project in the forefront."

Before you hire a publicist, make sure that person is known and respected by people in the media. You might call the entertainment editor of a magazine or the public relations department of a TV station and ask which publicists they would recommend. Once you sit down to talk to a publicist, you should try to ascertain just what kind of publicity program he intends to structure for your child.

"Once I'm hired as your child's publicist," says Story, "we will sit down and develop a campaign, what the child will talk about to the media. Then we go to the media. If it's a movie and the child is a new face, the media may want to screen the movie first. Then you set up the interview with the child and the press or the appearance on the show. It's then my job to prepare the child for this. I may set up a mock interview and ask the child some questions that they might be asked so the child is clear about what she should and should not talk about.

"Communication between a publicist and his client is essential. When I work with someone for a period of time, I become very much like a member of the family. That's why parents should make sure that the publicist's values are compatible with their own. They should also understand in advance exactly how that publicist is going to deal with their child. There is no one right way to do publicity. You have to create the direction based on the client you are handling. What is absolutely right for one young performer can be completely wrong for another."

Paying for Publicity

When you call a publicist for the first time, he will generally talk to you on the phone for a few minutes. If he thinks there is a reasonable chance that you can work together, he will probably ask you to come over to his office for a face-to-face meeting. Unlike attorneys, you should not have to pay a publicist any money for an initial interview. If someone does bill you for an initial meeting, I would certainly question that.

Although the cost of publicity varies greatly, the average fee at this time generally runs from $750 to $5,000 a month—plus expenses. Most publicists want new clients to commit for six months to a year. These terms maybe negotiable, depending on how well established the publicist is, how high his overhead is, and how badly he wants your child as a client. For example, one publicist's normal contract is for a year with a specific monthly retainer plus expenses. However, he occasionally will make exceptions.

"If a client has great potential but can't afford my regular fee for a year," *says Patricia Story, "I will sometimes sign her to a three-year deal for ten* *percent of everything she earns during that period. Of course, I let her convert back to the terms of my normal contract as soon as ten percent of her* *annual income starts surpassing my regular fee."*

In evaluating the cost of publicity, don't ever minimize the plus-expenses rider a publicist tacks onto her monthly fee. A publicist's expenses include postage, telephone calls, photocopying, and messengers. These kinds of standard operating expenses typically run from $200 to $500 a month. But the costs can go far beyond that, depending on how popular a child is and how much publicity a parent wants.

I've never thought of publicity as anything more than icing on the cake. Yet I know families who have borrowed money to hire publicists, only to be disappointed because they didn't get the results they had hoped for. It's important for parents to understand the value, as well as the limitations, of publicity.

Some parents seem to have the misguided notion that big-league publicists can guarantee a child the cover of *People* or an appearance on *The Late Show with David Letterman*. "Mothers and fathers who approach publicity that way are only fooling themselves," the late John Springer, one of the best publicists of the twentieth century, once told me. "No matter how good a publicist is, he can never offer any assurance that a child will appear on a particular show or magazine cover."

By now I hope you've come to realize that your child's acceptance or rejection in any show business situation can be based on all sorts of unpredictable factors. The producer of a TV show may not want your child as a guest because he doesn't like kids, or because the **ratings** were low the last time a child was featured—or for a hundred other reasons. "In signing a contract with a publicist," says Patricia Story, "you should do so with the knowledge that there are absolutely no guarantees." Good advice! But truthfully, I expect that any parent whose child is in a position to benefit from publicity would have learned long ago that in this business there are *never* any guarantees.

Ratings:

A complex survey system that measures the popularity of TV shows.

Putting Together a Support Team—
NOTES

- An accountant experienced in show business has a much better sense of what is a safe deduction for a performer to take in a given year.
- It is wise to consult an entertainment attorney whenever your child is asked to enter into a contractual agreement with an agent or a manager, unless that agreement is an unaltered standard union contract with no additions.
- Obtain information about work permits and state employment laws by contacting your state Department of Labor, Employment Standards Division; the Department of Social Services; or the SAG, AFTRA, or Equity office nearest you.
- Agency or management contracts—among the issues you should make sure you know:

    What is the length of the agreement?
    Which work will be commissioned?
    How much power are you giving away?
    How much money are you giving away?

- Save all of your receipts!
- When considering hiring a publicist, ask yourself: Is my child's role and/or performance special enough to attract significant media attention?
- In publicity as in show business, there are never any guarantees.

9

So Your Child Landed the Job: Now What?

If your child lands a role in a major film, TV, or theatrical production, everyone concerned will be excited. That's only natural. Still, the life of a professional show business child is not an easy one. With each new level of success come new expectations, new responsibilities, and new pressures—for your child, for yourself, and for the rest of your family.

I remember that I had to make quite an adjustment in my lifestyle when my daughter, Bonnie, landed her first major role—a part in an off-Broadway production at Joseph Papp's New York Shakespeare Festival. Most of my days were spent sitting around while rehearsals were going on. When Bonnie wasn't actually participating in the rehearsals, I had to make sure that she was keeping up with her schoolwork and getting a reasonable amount of rest. Sometimes rehearsals would run quite late: we often arrived home past midnight, feeling totally exhausted. As if that wasn't enough, I still had to attend to the needs of my other two children, including getting them off to school the next morning.

Of course, there was also a good side to all this. I was grati-
fied to be helping Bonnie do something that was really important to her. I was also learning a lot about the business, and that
was exciting, too. After a while I found that I had a lot in common with some of the other parents, and we became quite
friendly. Things became easier once all the mothers and fathers
got to know one another. We took turns staying at rehearsals, so
that each of us had some time during the day to attend to other
chores.

As I mentioned earlier, Bonnie was discovered without any
special effort on my part. I realized, however, that many of the
other parents had put a great deal of effort into furthering their
children's careers. I noticed that some of those mothers and fathers could hardly hold themselves back from coaching their children and making suggestions to the director and producer. I must
admit that more than once I had the urge to put my two cents in.
But I soon realized that this was not my job.

It's hard for some mothers and fathers to accept that they
are not the performers, nor are they the professionals who run the
show. Parents who butt in too much are sometimes trying to live
vicariously through their children. It's important for you not to let
such emotions erode your relationships with the professionals who
work with your child. According to *Annie* director Martin
Charnin:

---

*"A parent has to be secure enough to give up a certain amount of power
over her child in a working situation. She also has to accept that she may
not understand the reasons certain creative decisions are being made. The
way a child interprets a scene, for example, is not an area with which a
parent should concern herself. That kind of interference only confuses the*

child. A parent who questions a director's creative decisions similarly would be resentful if that director came to her and asked why her child sleeps in a room with ducks on the wall.

"What you have to remember is that you will always be your child's parent. On the other hand, a child's professional experiences are all transient. These experiences do make impressions. But when the show ends, the child will move on to another professional experience. Throughout all this you are still his mother or father."

To my mind, a good professional parent is one who helps her child further his career goals without sacrificing the child's personal growth. I'd like for you to understand just what to expect once your child starts working so that you can develop this kind of well-balanced approach. As in chapter 6, I've asked some respected colleagues to share their insights with us.

Rehearsals: Dealing with Long Hours and Unpredictable Situations

Parents often don't realize that when their child works on a project, there is usually a lot of waiting time. A child who is required to be on the **set** at 9:00 A.M. might not have anything to do until late that afternoon. And what about you? As the parent of a young performer, you can expect to spend the majority of your time sitting around, so you'd better bring a good book or some other diversion to occupy your time. Confesses Lisa Simon, *Sesame Street* producer-director:

Set:

An indoor location (often artificially constructed) where a scene takes place.

"I never realized how bored parents could get until my niece was on the show. My sister had come in from the suburbs at eight in the morning, but most of the time we don't start working with the kids until noon. I became so aware of my sister's irritation that I almost considered readjusting the whole schedule just to appease her. That incident made me aware of how long parents wait and how frustrated they can become."

Of course, waiting time can be very hard on children as well as parents. Just imagine a six-year-old child who has been sitting around for half a day waiting to shoot. Suddenly the producer says, "We're ready for you now. Let's do it." By that time, the child is cranky and wants to take a nap. It's part of your job as a parent to keep your child occupied and ready to perform. Still, I know from personal experience that if things aren't planned correctly by the professional staff, there isn't very much you can do.

When my son David was eight, he did a commercial for a well-known brand of fruit pies. During one part of the commercial David had to take a bite of a fruit pie—a really big bite. Unfortunately, that part of the commercial was shot at 2:00 P.M., after everyone had been fed a big, delicious lunch. Nobody bothered to tell me what was coming next, so I didn't stop David from stuffing himself. The results were almost disastrous.

Immediately after lunch the producer announced that they were ready to shoot the eating **scene**. David was brought onto the set and asked to take a great big bite of fruit pie. I don't know how many **takes** they did, but David had to eat a tremendous amount of pie in the course of the afternoon. The first few bites were fine. But by the time the shoot was over, David was pretty green.

Scene:

A section of a dramatic work taken by itself as a single piece of action.

Take:

A filmed or videotaped shot of a single piece of action. Frequently, several attempts may be required before the recording of a scene is accepted by a director.

As we were getting ready to leave, a representative from the pie company came up to David and said, "Guess what, David? I have a surprise for you. Here's a whole box of fruit pies for you to take home." David looked at the man and said, "I'm never going to eat another one of those things as long as I live."

Since commercial productions rarely last more than a day or two, any stress involved in rehearsing and shooting endless takes is short-lived. The rehearsal regimen for a Broadway show, on the other hand, can seem endless. During the week before a show opens, often there will be twelve-hour rehearsal days. As you get closer to opening night the tension can increase tremendously. Once the show begins performances, many directors still maintain a rigorous rehearsal schedule. Martin Charnin explains:

"As far as I'm concerned, rehearsals are an ongoing process. It takes x amount of time to get the show in front of an audience. Even after a show opens, the theater remains a living, open, breathing organism that must keep evolving. If the rehearsal process ends too early, the project can end up in

trouble. As a director, I consider myself an artist, and I never want to sign a painting until long after I think it's complete.

*"Some directors like to **freeze** a moment onstage early in the rehearsal process, but I tend to freeze things late. I like to keep on looking and finding new wrinkles. Since children often have a shorter concentration span, I try to keep them on their toes by constantly shifting things around throughout the rehearsals. The idea is to keep the whole rehearsal process as flexible as possible. In Annie, I would often reblock a scene just to keep the adventure going, knowing full well that I'd wind up with the original **blocking** in the end."*

Freeze:

In theater, the term used in rehearsal when a director decides that a particular scene will be portrayed exactly that way when the show opens.

Blocking:

The staging of the physical action in a scene.

As more and more children are used in professional situations, producers and directors are becoming increasingly aware of how to deal with their special needs. "Producers and directors can't treat a child the same way they treat an adult," observes producer Caryn Mandabach. "You have to make adjustments, even though it's not necessarily a question of children versus adult actors. Every actor needs special treatment. That's why sensitive professionals take each person's problem and deal with it on an individual basis."

As the producer of *The Cosby Show*, Caryn had the good fortune to be working with a man who was famous for his sensitivity to children. I happened to be present at a taping session where five-year-old Keshia Knight Pulliam fell down and hurt herself. Bill dealt with the situation in a fantastic way: He faked a fall and pretended to get hurt. Keshia made a quick recovery, and before long she was back into the scene again. I can't imagine what would have happened if someone without Bill Cosby's understanding of children tried to get Keshia up and working again. Nobody could have said to that five-year-old at that moment, "This is an important scene, and you've got to get up and do it right." If anyone had said that, they probably would have had no scene at all. As it was, Bill made Keshia smile, and she soon forgot about the incident completely.

Parents really can't predict how the people who work with their child will handle difficult or unusual situations. But as a rule, unless something is happening that threatens the well-being of your son or daughter, you would do well just to stay in the background and allow the professionals the autonomy to do things their way.

How Can You Help Without Interfering?

While producers and directors generally do not want mothers and fathers to contribute their creative input, parents do have an important role to play in professional situations. As one producer explains, "A parent's job is strictly this: to care for the emotional and physical health of her child and to support the producer in his effort to make the best show possible. Sometimes I hear a parent telling her child, 'This is just your job for now, honey. Later, there will be bigger and better things coming your way.' I don't like parents who are always dangling carrots in front of a child's face. I prefer the kind of parent who says, 'This is your job, and it's important to do it right.'"

In protecting your child's health, welfare, and mental stability, don't ever hesitate to speak up if you spot a dangerous situation or a situation in which your child is being asked to do something she is unable to do. If your daughter is on a **location** shoot and they have her sitting in a tree in the rain all day, talk to the producer about it or call your agent. If a director wants your son to ride a two-wheeled bicycle and he hasn't yet mastered that skill, it's up to you to step in and say, "He can't ride a bicycle." That kind of input is not interference; it's just being a good parent.

Location:

A place outside a studio where filming or videotaping is done.

Each child has his own needs and limitations—just as each producer has her own preferences when it comes to working with parents. Mothers and fathers who are aware of these differences are able to communicate their concerns more effectively. To help you better understand the needs of the professionals you work with, I've asked three respected producers for their contrasting points of view on how parents can help without interfering.

Sesame Street producer-director Lisa Simon understands that it's often necessary for parents to remain close by when their children are working. Still, she has come to the conclusion that many children perform better when their parents are out of the room:

"I don't want mothers and fathers on the studio floor when we're shooting because children often focus too much attention on their parents. A child may be more reticent to do something or look to his parent for an evaluation of his performance. Kids need to relate to the people they're working with, not to their parents.

"Personally, I don't even like parents to be in the building. I would rather have them come back at lunchtime and at the end of the day. But the woman who deals with parents on Sesame Street likes them to be available all day—just in case they're needed. There's a monitor set up so that parents can watch what's going on, but they are never allowed in the room where we're working. As creative professionals, we need that kind of autonomy."

Writer-producer Billy Van Zandt likes the space to work without parental interference:

*"Where we run into trouble with kids is when parents try to redirect the child. When we're on the set for a **runthrough** and we see it the way we want it, we then go back and do the rewrites based on that. We either like what we see or we tell the director that this is what we want fixed. Nothing drives us crazier as writer producers than to come in the next day and realize that the parents have directed the kid to do it in a totally different way because they think it will make the joke funnier. What usually happens in the next rewrite is that we cut the line."*

Runthrough:
An uninterrupted rehearsal with all scenes in the correct order.

We've seen some sharp differences in what producers Billy Van Zandt and Lisa Simon expect from parents. Each producer's approach is based on a combination of personal style and the special requirements of their particular projects. Lisa Simon, who also directs some episodes of *Sesame Street*, feels that since many of the children she works with have no professional experience, they are more likely to be distracted by their parents. Billy Van Zandt works on a number of projects every year—often with more seasoned young performers.

As the producer of many TV series, Caryn Mandabach has her own thoughts on parental involvement:

"If there's nothing wrong and everything is fine, the best thing a parent can do is keep to herself and just observe what's going on. That's not always easy. Let's face it—this can be a boring situation to find yourself in. You're spending days on end watching someone else work, and yet you have to be there. That's why I suggest that parents try to find something amusing with which to occupy themselves."

Whatever their differences, these three producers have much in common: each insists on his or her autonomy as a professional, and each is sensitive to the special needs of children.

Though all three producers make it a point to hire staffs who share that sensitivity, it's not always easy to find professionals who can both empathize with children and motivate them to give their best. As one producer observes:

"Sometimes I think that directors are frightened of pushing a child too hard. I think that you can ask a great deal of a child, as long as you're honest and gentle. I often see directors who are not afraid of adults but who are hesitant to really go for broke with a child. If I were a parent and I thought my son or daughter could handle the scene emotionally, I would give the director permission to go for it. I would say to the director, 'It's an upsetting scene for her, but don't worry—Kelly can take it.'"

As an agent, I try to be very sensitive to what's going on in a child's personal life. I would hesitate to send a child on a film about divorce, for example, if his parents are going through a particularly emotional separation. In other instances, however, I might feel that it would be good for a child to act out some of his feelings. I depend on parents to help me make these decisions, as do producers and directors when the child is on the job.

Understanding the Chain of Command: When to Talk and When to Listen

Parents often ask me, "Who do I talk to if my child has a problem in a working situation?" There is no simple answer that covers every instance. However, if you're in doubt, you can always ask your agent. If you have the right kind of agent, she will say, "This is something you should handle yourself," or "Go talk to the producer," or "I'll make a phone call and see if we can work it out." A good agent will always be as close as the nearest phone. It is her responsibility to help you deal with any problems that might come up. That's one reason why she receives 10 percent of your child's earnings.

In most productions there is a chain of command and someone in that hierarchy will be in charge of dealing with parents. Each time you arrive on the set of a new job, make it your business to find out who you should speak to about your child. On shows that regularly use a lot of children, such as *Sesame Street*, there is often a person who is directly responsible for the children. He or she would be the first one to see if your child needs lunch, a drink of water, or a nap. In most working situations, however, the person to speak to about your child's problems is the producer.

The decision of whether to go directly to the producer or to your agent first depends on the particular situation. I personally like a parent to let me decide whether she or I should speak to the producer. An agent develops a feel for these things, and it can't hurt to call and ask for her opinion. Still, each professional has her own preferences and point of view. Here are some of Caryn Mandabach's feelings on the subject:

"If there's a problem with money, I would always go right to the agent. However, if there is any problem with the director—if the director is being insensitive—I would speak to the producer about the director's attitude. Remember, the director is hired by, and is responsible to, the producer. If there's a problem with a tutor, or if a child didn't have a chance to nap, I would also go right to the producer."

Whomever she goes to first, a parent should always have recourse. No matter how important a job is or how well it pays, you should never allow anybody to abuse your child, either verbally or physically. I've had directors say things like this to a six-year-old child: "Listen, kid, shut your mouth, because you're going to make a lot of money on this." One commercial agent recalls an incident in which the parent of one of her clients was too intimidated to report the physical abuse of her child.

"Years ago a boy I was representing was hit on the head by a well-known actor during a commercial shoot—not once but twice! The child got hysterical, but the mother kept her mouth shut. The director eventually cut the scene from the commercial because the adult actor was obviously misbehaving beyond tolerable limits.

> *"This was probably the child's first major commercial, and the mother didn't want to rock the boat. Still, I was appalled to learn that this parent just sat there and allowed her child to be abused in this way. If your child is in any kind of clear and present danger, open your mouth immediately. Don't ever worry about his losing the job if you speak out."*

Whatever your problem, the last person to discuss it with is another mother. As I constantly have to tell parents, "Keep your ears open and your mouth shut." When you're sitting with a group of mothers and they're all discussing what's going on, that's a good time to listen—not talk. The more you can keep your ears open and your mouth shut, the better off you'll be. If you want to talk about the weather or Little League, great. But don't talk about your problems or about anything else that is going on in your child's career.

Parents have a tendency to sit around and gab about the three auditions their child has tomorrow or the two he did yesterday. Don't allow yourself to get caught up in this game of "Can You Top This" with other mothers and fathers. Perhaps your child is going on an audition that none of the other parents are aware of. If you start bragging, another parent might call up her agent and make her aware of the audition. Ultimately, that child may wind up landing the job.

On the other hand, if you hear someone mention an audition your child isn't on, call your agent immediately—but don't talk about it with any of the other parents. I don't like to see parents become sneaky or nasty about these things, but this is a competitive business and you don't want to blow any possible advantage.

Naturally, when you have an ongoing working situation, it's nice to become close with the other parents. Even here, I would avoid indulging in too much gossip. But sometimes, when there is a situation that affects all of the children, it may be advisable to take it up jointly with the producer. Caryn Mandabach found that rather than causing friction, this approach brought her closer to the parents she worked with on *The Cosby Show*:

"I had meetings with the parents where they collectively had a grievance of some kind. These discussions were productive for the most part. I had—both on an individual and on a collective basis—many open discussions with parents pertaining to their children and how the production was treating them in one way or another. Through this open communication I think we established a wonderful rapport. In certain respects we grew into a kind of family."

Because the type of project your child is working on plays such an important part in determining your course of action, I thought it would be profitable for us to explore some of the specifics that come up in various professional situations. Since I can't possibly cover every single contingency that might occur when your child starts to work, I'll focus on those issues that have the greatest impact on young performers and their parents.

On Camera: Studio vs. Location Work

The filming or videotaping of a commercial, film, or TV project can be accomplished in either one of two ways: in a simulated **studio** situation or in the real environment where the action is supposed to take place—that is, on location. A scene that is supposed to take place in a house, for example, might be filmed on a **soundstage**—on sets that are designed to look like the interior of a house. These **interiors** are re-created inside the studio. There, all the necessary sound equipment, makeup rooms, dressing rooms, and support facilities are under one roof. If that same scene were being shot on location, everyone would travel to a real house. All the necessary equipment would be transported and set up inside the house, while some rooms would serve as dressing rooms, makeup rooms, and the like. The people who actually live in that house would either be temporarily moved into a part of the house not used for the filming or moved out completely until the shoot was over.

Studio:

A soundproof indoor location where filming and/or recording is done.

Soundstage:

A soundproof room used for filming or videotaping motion pictures or television programs.

Interior:

The term used to describe any indoor setting in a film or TV production.

The same studio versus location options also apply to exterior or outdoor scenes, which can be shot either in a simulated studio environment or on actual locations. Although there are many similarities between studio and location work, there are also some important differences, particularly for the children who are performing and their parents.

When you work in a studio, there is usually a lot less space, so things can become pretty tight. But when you're outside—in a park, for example—there is lots of room for a child to either study his lines, do his homework, or relax when he is not actually working. In this more spacious environment, actors are free to move around as they please as long as they are within shouting distance when the director wants them.

Studio shoots are a lot more confining and often a lot less fun for children. Even when the location is a private home rather than a park or beach, you can usually go outside when you're not filming. But if a child's first shoot is in a studio, it can be a very long day with not much to do. In any case, it's always wise to bring along a book, a game, or something else to occupy your child while he's waiting to shoot.

Sometimes my clients land assignments on locations that are entertaining and interesting places in and of themselves. Several years ago, one of my young actors was working on a film that was shot in the Fiji islands. That child and his mother lived, ate, and slept on a ship. I guess you can't hope for a more remote location than that. They both had what amounted to an exotic vacation.

I was never lucky enough to be sent to a tropical island when my own children were working. I did, however, have a whole range of experiences accompanying them to shoots. One thing I learned was that the success of any particular project had no relation whatsoever to the amount of fun I had on the set. I recall one particularly boring day when my son David did a commercial for a toy company. Although neither of us had a very good time that day, that toy commercial turned out to be one of the most lucrative, highly visible projects my son ever worked on.

David's part in the commercial was to construct a model toy. All day long he sat at a desk in a studio, putting one piece on top of the next and saying his one line. Because David had to put the toy together perfectly, there were any number of things that could—and did—go wrong: the piece didn't fit exactly right; the lighting wasn't perfect; the line reading was a little off.

Meanwhile, there I was, sitting all the way on the other side of the studio, watching my son put this thing together and take it apart over and over again. My main job that day was to escort David to the bathroom and make sure that he stayed clean. Basically, that was a terribly long and boring day for both of us. But then again, not many young performers are in a position to take only fascinating assignments or those that are shot at exotic locations. As the parent of a working child, you have to be prepared for the worst—even as you try to help him land the best and most interesting roles.

Broadway: Openings and Closings

Parents of children who work in the theater think that landing a Broadway show is the end of the rainbow. In some respects, that's not an inaccurate perception. But there is also a flip side: Broadway shows are more likely to close after one night than any other type of theatrical production. Off-Broadway shows are usually designed to run for a specified period of time. Road companies are put together only after a show has proven itself and the producers are confident that it's going to succeed. But a Broadway show can run for one day, two weeks, or five years. Don't forget the *Miracle Worker* saga from chapter 2. It never opened at all.

I've seen children put a lot of time into rehearsing for a Broadway show, only to have the show close after one performance. These are multimillion-dollar productions that usually require weeks of long rehearsals. Most Broadway shows preview for a week or two, and everybody builds up to the excitement of opening night. For days people talk about what they are going to wear to the opening night party. Finally, the big night arrives.

Imagine the scenario: Everyone is standing around in their tuxedos and evening dresses; they all feel good about the opening performance and are hoping for a long, successful run. Then the reviews come in and they're awful. At that point the producers of the show sometimes decide to fold their tents, and that's it!

It's tough enough for adults to handle this kind of disappointment, but it's ten times harder for a child to understand why something he loves and has worked so hard for is dying without ever really having a life. I've had to explain to my young clients that when certain powerful people don't like a show or decide not to invest any more money in it, that show will have to close.

Normally, when a show closes abruptly, I'll call the child into my office for a talk. "You did a terrific job," I'll tell him, "and people will remember that. Let's put this aside now and start working on the next project." Sometimes the blow is softened because the reviews have singled that particular child out for praise. But here again your handling of the situation is probably the single most important factor in how well your child will be able to bounce back.

Touring Companies: You and Your Child on the Road

When your child is selected to be part of a touring company for a major theatrical production, you and he will generally be asked to make a six-month commitment to that show. Depending on the itinerary, you can spend as long as several months or as little as one day in a given city. Some tours travel strictly by plane, flying the entire company from one major city to another, while other touring companies are transported by bus. As Martin Charnin observes:

"Touring companies become like little countries—worlds unto themselves. At one point we had five road companies of Annie *on tour, and I visited*

each one of them frequently. When I arrived in some small town, I'd find seventy-five people all alone in their own little microcosm. It always seemed to me that, in time, each road company became like a sanctuary that was very separate from the rest of the world. I thought of each road company as an island that surfaced, and then disappeared when it wasn't performing. From my perspective they all had to be carefully monitored, attended to, and cared for."

While you're on tour you and your child will be living in hotels and out of trunks. This change in lifestyle can be difficult at first, though most of my young clients and their parents seem to have a wonderful time once they get used to it. Touring is a good way to travel and see the country. One touring mother told me that the major decision she had to make every day was which restaurant she and her daughter were going to eat at that night. "I don't know how I'm going to deal with washing dishes after this," she confessed.

School: Continuing Your Child's Education

When a performing child begins to work regularly, it's up to the parents to make sure that he continues to receive a good, well-rounded education. There's not much of a problem if a child has to miss a day or two of school to audition or to shoot an occasional commercial. But the situation can become a good deal more complex if he has to miss regular classes for extended periods of time.

Children who land roles in a long-term production or who work regularly in a variety of projects have to juggle two full-time careers. Young performers have to maintain the same rigorous rehearsal schedule as their adult counterparts. At the same time they are legally required to maintain a full scholastic load. I've asked Alan Simon, president of On Location Education, the best-known tutoring service for professional children in the performing arts as well as child athletes and children of celebrities, to talk about how his company is utilized:

"Parents want to keep their children A-level students as well as A-level actors, and they come to On Location Education for half that equation. We maintain a roster of teachers who are qualified to teach practically anything to any age at a moment's notice. Because of the nature of the industry, our school is fluid and flexible to work around rehearsal and performance schedules, but in every other way we try to give the child a superior school experience."

One of the first things Alan Simon's company does when working with a young performer is to contact the child's school and find out what subjects the child is taking.

"Initially, I try to show a school that I want to fully cooperate with them and make their job easier. I will call them and say, 'On Location Education is representing XYZ Production Company. This child will be out of school for this period of time. Please give me some general guidelines and indicate where you want the child to be scholastically when he or she returns to class.'

"If a school is willing to cooperate with me—and most are—things can go very smoothly. The school provides books, guidelines, and homework assignments. They also tell me if they want the tutor to handle testing or

whether they prefer to deal with it themselves. In some cases, a school trusts us completely and turns the child over to our jurisdiction. We are given permission to both test and grade that child. We send everything back by fax or e-mail, and the school accepts it.

"Unfortunately, not all school systems are this cooperative. Remember, you're asking a school system to operate in a situation that is not normal, so their resistance is understandable. I often have to work hard to build a relationship of trust. I have to convince a school system that the child will continue to receive a quality education, and that it won't cost them anything in terms of manhours and additional money. As more schools learn to deal with the special needs of professional children, they are becoming more cooperative.

"Basically, the decision to accommodate a working child is up to the individual principals and guidance counselors in a particular school. If they see that the work is getting done, there is usually no problem. But sometimes a school just doesn't want to cooperate. At that point a parent has to decide to either enroll her child in a different school or pull him out of the production."

Although the laws vary from state to state, most jurisdictions require a tutor for children who work for three or more days on one set. If a road company of a theatrical production includes children, there has to be at least one tutor along to help them keep up with their studies. Both California and New York have very comprehensive laws involving working conditions for children. In other parts of the country, union regulations are often more comprehensive than state laws.

SAG's regulations (see the appendix) regarding the education of and work regulations for performing children will give you a good general overview of what is expected. If you want more specific information about particular state or union guidelines, contact your nearest SAG, AFTRA, or Equity office, or the Department of Labor in your state.

Some parents have turned to homeschooling for their children when the public or private school has been unwilling to cooperate with the demands of our business. There are some excellent homeschooling programs available. Many utilize the Internet. This can give a family the flexibility of arranging schoolwork around auditions and performances. But a parent then must wear two hats, and that can be tough. If you are already having a struggle with your child over cleaning his or her room or doing homework, imagine the conflicts that can erupt when you are the full-time teacher as well. Alan Simon advises:

"If parents choose the homeschooling route, it is important that they do it in a legitimate way. By legitimate, I mean done through your local school system, whereby you enroll your child in school and do the homeschooling program with the support of the local school district. Whether it be a religion-based program or not, get the support of the establishment. This will allow you to obtain a work permit when your child is hired for a job. It is much more difficult, and sometimes even impossible, to get a work permit if your child has no connection with a school system."

Work permits are becoming the norm. They are required in New York and California and virtually every other state, as well as in many Canadian provinces. In New York, the district must confirm that the child is in good standing, and the principal or district supervisor must sign a letter stating that fact. In California, a child must show that he is performing at a 'C' or better level in every subject in order to obtain a permit. Nearly every other state has similar restrictions.

No matter what the applicable state or union regulations are, I feel that parents should assume the major responsibility for their son's or daughter's education. As your child gets older and her academic needs become more specialized, it can become more difficult to maintain a balance between school and career. If, for example, your child wants to take an advanced biology course, it may be next to impossible for her to keep up with her laboratory assignments. At that point you and your child will have a tough choice to make. As a parent, it's your job to recognize your child's cutoff point and to help her establish appropriate goals and priorities.

I have seen cases in which a child's education was sacrificed for the sake of professional advancement, but I also know quite a few young performers who adeptly juggle school and work. Many of my present and former clients now attend excellent universities, such as Yale, Cornell, Princeton, and Vassar. Some of them did miss quite a number of classes when they were younger, but obviously they were able to keep up with the work.

Tutoring can sometimes make the difference between a passing or failing grade for a child. When David Krumholtz was hired for a TV project as a teenager, his math skills were in trouble. He barely got the work permit. We requested a tutor who was strong in the area of math. He and the tutor focused on that area but still kept up on his other work. The good news is that he returned to his home school when he finished the series and passed his math Regents exams. Without the tutoring, he was in danger of failing.

Many of my older clients manage to maintain excellent grades in college without abandoning their performing careers. Their professors usually allow them to take a week off from time to time, as long as they keep up with the required work. Sometimes performers who want to accept particularly lengthy or demanding projects decide to take an entire semester off from college and resume their studies the following term. This type of scheduling may not be conventional. But then again, most successful young performers are extraordinarily bright and capable.

A growing number of progressive educational institutions now encourage their students to obtain practical life and work experience—often for academic credit. My client Ramzi Khalaf will be graduating from New York University a semester early because of the credits he received for his work in show business. I'm not suggesting that colleges should necessarily accept acting in a film or play as a substitute for formal studies. Nevertheless, working in show business can be a highly enriching educational experience. Where else can a young person receive this unique opportunity to earn good money while visiting exciting places and meeting interesting people? I don't think it's stretching the point to say that such experiences can have as much bearing on a young person's overall education as anything she might learn in a classroom.

The Home Front: What About the Rest of the Family?

In chapter 2, we talked about how important a supportive and flexible family is at every stage of a young performer's career. In certain respects there are greater pressures on a child's family as he becomes more successful.

If you go out on the road with your child or accompany him to rehearsals every day, it's easy for other family members to feel neglected or become envious. Your husband may not be in love with the idea that you're never home to prepare dinner while your other children can become resentful that you are paying so much attention to the one child who is a performer.

A smart, sensitive parent will try to find some way to make the rest of the family feel a part of the experience. In many families it's the mother who accompanies the performing child. Under these circumstances, you don't want the rest of the kids to feel that they have lost Mommy or that show business has taken Mommy away from them. Here are some suggestions that can help you avoid these difficulties.

If there are several children in the family, and you and Jason are on the road, have each brother and sister come one at a time—to spend a week or two touring with you. You might also have your husband or another relative take your place so that you can spend some time at home with the rest of the family. Children who perform in major productions often get to meet famous people and travel to interesting places. If a tour goes on for a long time and you plan it right, everyone can share in the excitement. If you plan well, the whole family might be able to join you for a part of their summer vacation. Normally, transportation and rooms for you and your child are paid for. Between this and your child's salary, there should be enough money available to include the entire family in this unique experience.

When a mother travels with a young performer, a supportive father can really help keep the family together. Single parents often enlist the aid of a grandparent or aunt. In some cases, the parent decides that the most practical course is to take the other children along. However you decide to handle the situation, you have to make a special effort to help the rest of the family keep things in perspective. TV producer Caryn Mandabach offers the following well-considered advice:

"My sense of this is that the parent should explain to the other children that this particular child has entered into a performing career at a young age and the family is doing what they can to help him. Because a parent loves her children, she assists each of them in their career or profession. 'One day,

when you want to get into a profession,' I would tell the other children, 'we will be there to help you. No matter what you do, your parents will always stand behind you. Just because your sister is famous doesn't mean that you're any less special to me. I'm just as proud of you for who you are.'"

You may recall that I talked about the Dieffenbach family in chapter 2. They're the family with five children—three who are interested in the business and two who are not. As I mentioned, the parents are equally supportive of all the children, as the children are of one another. Now I'd like you to hear some excerpts from an interview I conducted with another family in a similar situation. MacKenzie Mauzy is a fourteen-year-old girl from North Carolina. She appeared for two years on the soap opera *The Guiding Light* as the character Lizzy Spaulding. She has recently been cast as Sara Crewe, the lead, in the new musical *A Little Princess*. MacKenzie has a brother and sister who are just as attractive as she is but have absolutely no interest in performing. MacKenzie, her mother, Kim, and I spoke recently.

NANCY CARSON: How did your brother and sister react
    when you started to be pretty successful in the business?
MACKENZIE MAUZY: They were both really supportive.
    My sister is usually pretty excited when I get something,
    but my brother gets a little nervous that he won't be able
    to do the things he likes to do. My sister rides horseback
    and my brother plays lacrosse and football. They come to
    all my shows so I try to go to their things, too.
NANCY CARSON: Kim, how do you handle it?
KIM MAUZY: We're really, really busy. It takes both of us
    to do it. If my husband Corky wasn't supportive, we

couldn't make it all happen. I have really focused kids. My daughter Shelton wants to go to the Olympics with her horse, and my son Courtney lives and breathes sports. All three know exactly what they want to do, and they all knew it at a very young age. Basically Corky and I are spending this season of our lives helping them fulfill their dreams.

NANCY CARSON: MacKenzie, how do you handle being separated from half of your family and your friends when you go off to do a job?

MACKENZIE MAUZY: We stay in touch by phone and e-mail.

NANCY CARSON: When you were on *The Guiding Light* you were pretty visible. How did you talk about it to your friends?

KIM MAUZY: She didn't tell anybody.

MACKENZIE MAUZY: Yes, I did. I told my best friends, and my teachers knew, so it kind of just filtered out. Some people didn't believe it was me, so they'd come up and ask me. I just didn't make a big deal about it.

NANCY CARSON: Did it feel good? Did it feel weird?

MACKENZIE MAUZY: I don't mind that people know. I just don't want them to think of me as different from everyone else. I just act normal. It's kind of the same as if you're good at basketball or football. I try to think of it that way.

NANCY CARSON: How do you keep her normal, Kim?

KIM MAUZY: You know, I don't know. She doesn't like to stand out and be different. I know that sounds weird, because she's a performer. Until this year no one at school knew that she could sing. Then she was in the school musical, so they found out. She's much more nervous performing for the people at home that she cares about. She's fine when she's not MacKenzie. She just doesn't like to be a showoff.

MACKENZIE MAUZY: Doing shows does help me gain more confidence to perform in front of people I know.

NANCY CARSON: Do you try to include the whole family in the show business experience?

KIM MAUZY: Her brother and sister amaze me. Every experience has been wonderful for the whole family. We homeschooled everybody the two years that we did *The Guiding Light*. We had a blast exploring New York City. We saw tons of plays and museums and went all over Central Park. I think it's hardest for Corky and me because we're best friends as well as husband and wife. The kids truly understand the concept of following their dreams because they each have one.

MACKENZIE MAUZY: I don't get caught up in the glamour and money of it. I also don't dwell on the things I don't get. I do it because I love it. My motto is, "If there's nothing to prove, there's nothing to lose."

Last weekend I flew to California to see MacKenzie Mauzy star as Sara Crewe in the new musical *A Little Princess*. She was brilliant. As she took her bow the audience jumped to its feet, and the applause just wouldn't stop. MacKenzie has everything it takes to be a star. She's wonderfully talented. She's beautiful. She has supportive parents. And, most of all, she wants it more than anything else in the world. At fifteen she seems well on her way.

Each day I see at least one new person in my office. I want

nothing more than for that person to be my next star. I know that it's possible. I've seen it happen many times in my twenty-six years as an agent. I hope that this book has helped you to decide whether this is a journey that you and your family are prepared to take. Are *you* "raising a star"?

Appendix

Performers' Unions

Screen Actors Guild *www.sag.org*
NYC (212) 944-1030
L.A. (323) 954-1600

American Federation of Television and Radio Artists
www.aftra.org
NYC (212) 532-0800
L.A. (323) 634-8100

Actors' Equity Association *www.actorsequity.org*
(212) 869-8530

Additional Web Resources

Publications
www.backstage.com
www.showbusinessweekly.com
www.variety.com
www.broadway.com
www.playbill.com

Breakdowns, Sides, and Screenplay Access for Actors
www.actorsaccess.com

Child Performer Information
www.labor.state.ny.us/child
www.minorcon.org

Sample Résumé

When putting together a résumé, bear in mind that it is most likely that the person reviewing it will be looking at many other résumés at the same time. The résumés should be laid out in a simple, easy-to-read format and be limited to one page. Do not include dates of performances. Unlike most business résumés, acting credits should be listed according to significance, not date.

PERFORMER'S NAME
Union Affiliation (if any)

Contact Information:

Parent's Name and Phone Number or

Agent/Manager Name and Phone Number

Height:

Weight:

Hair Color:

Eye Color:

Date of Birth:

Vocal Range (*if a singer*):

In the following categories, list name of production, role played, production company

THEATER

FILM

TELEVISION

COMMERCIALS

PRINT WORK

RADIO

TRAINING (*dance, voice, acting*)

List name of school or teacher, type of training, length of study.

SPECIAL SKILLS

List athletics, languages and dialects, musical instruments, etc.